Julie M. Creus

Adventures in Fabric
La Todera Style

Sew 20 Projects for You & Your Home

stashBOOKS®

an imprint of C&T Publishing

Text copyright © 2014 by Julie M. Creus

Photography and Artwork copyright © 2014 by C&T Publishing, Inc.

Publisher: Amy Marson

Creative Director: Gailen Runge

Art Director/Book Designer: Kristy Zacharias

Editor: Karla Menaugh

Technical Editors: Susan Hendrickson and Carolyn Aune

Production Coordinator: Rue Flaherty

Production Editor: Katie Van Amburg

Illustrator: Tim Manibusan

Photo Assistant: Mary Peyton Peppo

Photo Stylist: Lauren Toker

Styled photos by Nissa Brehmer, unless otherwise noted; Instructional photos by Diane Pedersen, unless otherwise noted

Published by Stash Books, an imprint of C&T Publishing, Inc., P.O. Box 1456, Lafayette, CA 94549

Library of Congress Cataloging-in-Publication Data

Creus, Julie M. (Julie Marie), 1967-

 Adventures in fabric : La Todera style : sew 20 projects for you & your home / Julie M. Creus.

  pages cm

 ISBN 978-1-60705-962-2 (soft cover)

1. Soft sculpture. 2. Sewing. 3. House furnishings. 4. Dress accessories. I. Title.

 TT925.C74 2014

 746--dc23

                  2014009336

Printed in China

10 9 8 7 6 5 4 3 2 1

When I first met Julie Creus, she was participating in one of my workshops at Houston Quilt Festival. She stood out from the many workshop students because she presented me with a unique present—a carefully washed and ironed collection of shirt stripes bound together with a buttoned cuff. These charity shop finds were of many color combinations, some fine, some wonderfully bold.

I love recycled and found materials and used this collection in a quilt of patched stripes. The perception she showed alerted me to her imaginative use of prints.

I also began to tune into her genius for using prints for three-dimensional objects in a witty and aesthetic way.

I'm delighted she is sharing this talent with us all in her first book, and I have no doubt it will reach a large and appreciative audience of textile lovers. It is thrilling and informative for me to see how she uses my prints, revealing quite a new insight into each fabric she uses.

— *KAFFE FASSETT*

Julie Creus's delightful and ingenious way of playing with fabrics gives an imaginative, bold, and new look on color, shape, and form. Julie's original projects make me, as a fabric artist, feel proud of the way she incorporates my fabrics into her charming works of art.

— *BRANDON MABLY, THE KAFFE FASSETT COLLECTIVE*

Acknowledgments

To Cecilia Koppmann in Argentina, for her support and encouragement early on when La Todera was just an idea.

To Margaret Travis, who most generously shared all of her knowledge about the pattern business and got me started in my dream job of "pattern designer."

To my pals in the Orlando Modern Quilt Guild—thanks for putting up with my crazy projects, helping to try them, and cheering me along the way!

Many thanks to all of the generous companies that contributed supplies for this book—you've never seen someone so excited to see the UPS man every day!

And to all the wonderful folks at C&T who encouraged me every step of the way with this book! Most especially, my editor Karla Menaugh, with whom I was so fortuitously paired!

Wherever this journey takes us, I'll always have a place in my heart for all of you!

Dedication

This book is dedicated to my family—

My ever-so-encouraging husband, Santiago, who has such amazing MacGyver skills and impeccable taste. (And Argentine good looks to boot!) He is sooo patient about my crafty messes. Although one afternoon, after a particularly rabid day of crafting, he threatened to help me clean up my scraps on the living room floor—with a *leaf blower.* ...

My two über creative, smart, and patient children, Olivia and Liam, who are also the best helpers in the world. My business truly wouldn't be where it is today without them.

My mom, who taught me—an incorrigible student at first—to sew. And she supported *all* of my creative endeavors, from my first crayon "mural" on the kitchen floor at age two, to allowing all my crazy, messy childhood craft experiments, to helping me sew models for my patterns and talking up my patterns and fabric to anyone within earshot. :)

Table of Contents

Acknowledgments 3

Introduction 6

The Basics 8

About the Author 142

Resources 143

FOR THE LIVING AREA 17

18
Harlequin Star
Pillow Chair

24
Biscornu
Pillow

30
Malaysian
Mini Mat

36
Folded
Wall Flowers

FOR THE SEWING ROOM 61

62
Peacock
Pincushion

68
Ladybug
Pincushion

72
Kissing Flowers
Needle Case

78
Cloisonné
Catch-All Bowl

FOR THE HOLIDAYS 105

106
Lavish Lantern
Ornament

112
Puffy Tabletop
Christmas Trees

118
Furoshiki
Gift-Card Box

FOR THE DINING AREA   43

44	50	56
Lily Pad Centerpiece	Plumeria Placemat	Peep Show Hexies Coaster Set

JUST FOR YOU   85

86	92	98
Gum-Wrapper Weave Fabric Cuff	Zaftig Zinnia Brooch	Water Lily Brooches

FOR THE KIDS' AREA   123

124	130	138
Grabby Tabs Ball	Llama Mama and Baby	Butterfly Bunting

Projects

Introduction

My mom recently sent me a box of things she's saved—drawings and things I'd made as a kid. In it was a spiral-bound stack of notecards filled with instructions and illustrations for kids' craft projects—my first crafty book!

It brought me down memory lane of the *hours* I'd spend at the public library, almost magnetically drawn to the craft-book section. There was a certain series of books I particularly admired—*The Family Creative Workshop.* I'd check them out a tall stack at a time, over and over, studying the pictures and the way the authors communicated the craft instructions and how the book designer pulled all of the photos, illustrations, and copy together to achieve a cohesive book design. There was a huge range of crafts in those books. It wasn't a certain craft that intrigued me; it was the communication of those ideas. A book just seemed the most

genius way to communicate to a limitless audience through strategic photos and carefully written and edited instructions!

I remember a certain vacation spent at my grandmother's condo. "Red Gram" took me to a store with an office supply section, and I scoured the options for a book format—the spiral-bound notecard stack. Although I didn't fill up every one of those cards with crafts, I see that I must have spent the greater part of that trip on my grandmother's porch, writing down ideas and drawing illustrations in felt-tip pens! Gram was an innovator herself—I still have the homemade patterns she invented for a special neck pillow and for "petticoat pants" to wear under skirts to keep your undies from showing. Because of her own creativity, she was very supportive of me, and I remember her taking my project very seriously. :)

"Red Gram," who fostered my love of making books

Gram's parents, Annie and Michael. Family legend has it that Annie wasn't crazy about that photo and thought it needed flowers, so she painted them on the photo! She was a super flower fan. Red Gram, too. (Me three! My first pattern was a fabric flower.)

So there was the love of craft books. Then I followed a boyfriend into the graphic design program at college. The boyfriend didn't last, and neither did my graphic design career—I was bored designing catalog pages for others! Not to worry. The graphic design skills would serve me later.

I've always been fascinated with three-dimensional fabric projects—biscuit quilts, softies, folded fabric rugs, fabric flowers, things like that. There's just something almost … rebellious about making fabric do what you never thought it could! In fact, that's the basis of my business, La Todera Sewing and Craft Patterns. When I started it, there was really no other company devoted to fabric manipulation. I had a niche!

My pattern subjects are things I like—flowers, butterflies, and unusual animals. The subjects themselves come from the heart. I figure that if I design what I love, that will surely shine through and someone else will appreciate it.

Perhaps as a side effect of studying graphic design, I'm obsessed with defining the essence of things, distilling an object down to the minimum elements for that object to still be recognizable. Then I set about identifying and re-creating the elements of that subject in fabric. What is it exactly that makes a zinnia a zinnia? Thick, rounded petals; graduated color; a round, layered center bud. What is the minimum sum of details that make a peacock a peacock? Wedge-shaped feathers in a fan shape, a slim body ending in a beak, and a "head dress."

Then add in a bit of rebellion. Gotta have something different—something you can't buy, something in a scale you've never seen before, such as the 6″ Zaftig Zinnia Brooch (page 92); or colorway, such as Plumeria Placemat in crazy patterns (page 50). Maybe just a cool little something in a customized colorway, like the versatile Furoshiki Gift-Card Box (page 118).

Adventures in Fabric—La Todera Style is the book I always wanted to buy. There are a few sewing books out there with fabric manipulation techniques, but mostly for clothing. Or perhaps there was only one technique to be learned.

I'm leaving it all on the dance floor with this book. Every project has a special technique I've never seen anywhere else. All of these projects are want-able, gift-able items that I've been saving especially for this dream book of mine. I hope these projects light your fire for experimenting with fabric, too!

The Basics

Choosing Fabrics

Buy what you like, whatever catches your eye! Don't be intimidated by a large selection in a store. Trust your gut and buy the colors and prints that speak to you.

Having a large stash doesn't have to be expensive. Fabric goes on sale all the time; this is when you can stock up on basics like muslin and solids. Half yards are usually enough to make smaller projects. They also are easier to iron, fold, and cut into (as opposed to a 6-yard length!).

I happen to be a sucker for saturated, bright colors. But if that's not your thang, no problem. The "theories" in this chapter apply to you, too!

TONALS

You'll notice that when a certain shape is emphasized—the body of the Peacock Pincushion (page 62) or the shell of the Ladybug Pincushion (page 68)—I've chosen a tonal print. Tonals are printed with several variations of the same color or with subtle color differences. By choosing one of these, you notice the form first, then the color. There are cases when you don't want the shape of your piece and the design of the fabric competing— for example, a high-contrast print would detract from the shape of the petal, so you wouldn't choose it for a flower.

Interesting tonals are harder to find than you'd imagine. So stock up when you see some you like. In fact I based my fabric lines on this principle. I couldn't find them, so I designed them (Photochrome Petals and A Closer Look for Clothworks). Another go-to group of saturated, yet subtly "fluctuating" tonals I love is the Palette collection by Marcia Derse.

SOLIDS

Solid fabrics will accomplish the same thing as tonals, though read as "flatter," and thus I find them a bit more difficult to work with (counterintuitive, I know.)

Another thing about solids is that they seem to highlight all the little flaws in your sewing. That said, if the stitching is part of your design—let's say you are embroidering something on the fabric—then solids are a good choice since they will highlight your stitching.

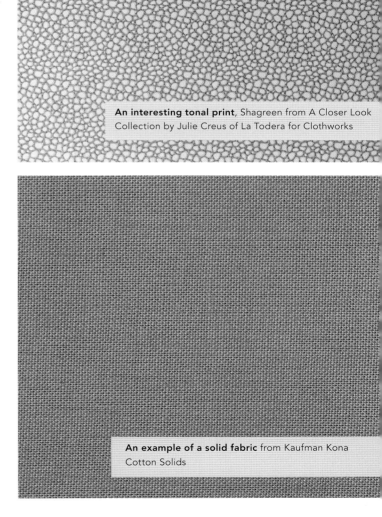

An interesting tonal print, Shagreen from A Closer Look Collection by Julie Creus of La Todera for Clothworks

An example of a solid fabric from Kaufman Kona Cotton Solids

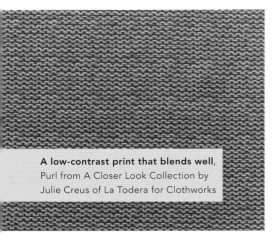

A low-contrast print that blends well, Purl from A Closer Look Collection by Julie Creus of La Todera for Clothworks

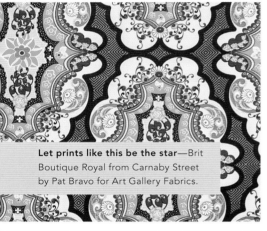

Let prints like this be the star—Brit Boutique Royal from Carnaby Street by Pat Bravo for Art Gallery Fabrics.

I love irregular dots, like Sunspots by Amy Butler for Westminster/Free Spirit.

PRINTS

As far as prints go, there are sooo many to choose from that it can be mind boggling. Luckily, people seem to have stronger reactions to prints than to other types of fabrics, so it's easier to get a gut reaction to follow when shopping.

Low-Contrast Prints

My favorite large prints are ones that don't have a huge fluctuation in value. Take the Kaffe Fassett Suzani print, which I used in the Grabby Tabs Ball (page 124). Hot pink, hot red, bright turquoise, and bright green. Seems like a contradiction, but all of the colors are similar in value. How to tell if a fabric has contrasting values? Take a quick snapshot and turn it to black and white. If you see a big difference in the gray scales, then the fabric has a higher contrast. Does it look flat? Then the colors have similar values.

It's not a hard-and-fast rule, but I find these certain fabrics with low contrast in values to be more "usable" in fabric manipulation projects, and I tend to gravitate toward them.

High-Contrast Prints

High-contrast prints don't always marry well with other fabrics. I often save them for when a project calls for only one fabric. That way the print can be the star. Or if another fabric is required, I may make it a tonal to create a contrast in the sections of the design. See, for example, the Folded Wall Flowers (page 36).

I don't happen to be a huge fan of white in large prints. It seems to immediately cause a lot of contrast within a print, making it especially difficult to pair with any of the fabrics in my stash!

Stripes and Polka Dots

Can't get enough. Just can't get enough (like the song!). Stripes are incredibly versatile. They can create contrast just by changing the direction of the same fabric. Polka dots are fresh and familiar at the same time. Same rule goes here as for any prints—low-value contrasts are your friend.

ON COMBINING FABRICS

Working with fabric is a bit different from other mediums. A painter can tweak a color by adding a contrasting wash on top or some other method. Sewists have to choose well from the beginning or be willing to do a lot of unsewing!

Here are some color theory and design principles that are bound to help you make successful projects:

- If you want to make adjoining pieces "pop," pick contrasting colors, markedly lighter or darker fabrics, or small prints to go with larger prints. Or combine these concepts.

- 3D projects are all about details. Look at the proportions of the detail. If you're going to be using a fabric just for a detail, don't judge whether it will work by putting two bolts of fabric next to each other. Cut a small piece of one and set it next to a larger piece, in approximate proportions to how those fabrics will figure in your project.

- My kids' kindergarten teacher used to say, "To color a small area, use a small brush; a large area, a large brush." This applies to choosing fabrics for 3D projects as well. For a small-detail piece, pick a small print, tonal, or solid. For a large area, you can use a large print.

- Of course, for every rule there is an exception. If a large fabric would provide the perfect detail in your project, by all means fussy cut it and use it! Just make sure it looks intentional.

- Stepping back is a good idea. Literally or with a photo. Take a phone photo in daylight. Are you happy with the combo? Flannel design walls are great for pinning things to look at from a distance. Find one in a neutral color—gray or camel. Kaffe Fassett has some amazing gridded gray flannel made for this purpose (see Resources, page 143). If a color combo really isn't "singing" for you, leave it for the day and come back later with fresh eyes. (I've always loved that saying of "fresh eyes." Somehow it makes me think of the sprinklers coming on in the produce section in the grocery store, making all of those fruits and vegetables look dewy and plump again after a day of bright lights and manhandling by store clerks and customers.)

- That said, there is no perfect color, nor a perfect fabric print. Only *amazing combinations*!

Construction Techniques

Learning a few key techniques will help make all of your projects successful, durable, and professional looking.

HAND SEWING

Backstitch

This stitch is essential if you are gathering or otherwise putting a lot of tension on your thread. Begin sewing by knotting the thread and taking a small stitch. Then reinsert the needle close to the knot and continue sewing. This stitch is also used at the end of a row of stitches to reinforce a knot.

Running Stitch

The simplest of sewing stitches. With this stitch, it's easy to pull the thread and gather your fabric.

Ladder Stitch

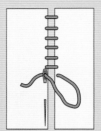

An invisible closure for an opening, such as one left for turning and stuffing.

Whipstitch

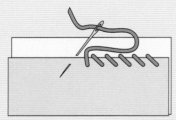

Used to close an opening in a project where the stitches won't be seen or where the ladder stitch would be too difficult, such as applying the tiny yo-yos in the center of the Plumeria Placemats (page 50). The whipstitch is faster and easier than the ladder stitch.

Unsewing

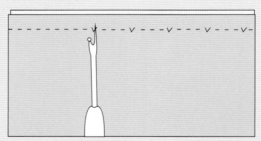

The best (fastest and neatest) way to "unsew" is to use a seam ripper to sever every fourth stitch on the reverse side of your seam. Turn your work over, pull out the top thread, and then remove the short threads remaining on the back of your work.

Bury Ends of Thread

Burying the ends of your thread serves two purposes. First, it makes your project look neater. Second, since you won't be trimming the thread right next to the knot, your knot will be less likely to come undone! After taking a small stitch and knotting your thread, reinsert the needle into your project and bring it out some distance away from the knot, leaving the excess thread inside your project. Trim the thread close to the fabric's surface.

KNOTS

Square Knot

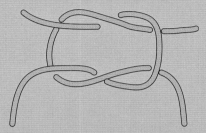

A square knot is made by crossing two ends and then threading one end through the loop formed twice. This knot is used in the first step of a bow, to finish the end of a cord, or as the basis of a surgeon's knot (at right).

Surgeon's Knot

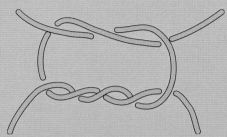

A surgeon's knot is perfect when you need a knot that will withstand a lot of tension. Start by making an additional pass when tying the first throw of a square knot. The additional turn provides more friction and will reduce loosening while the second half of the knot is tied. Wax the thread to increase your grip even more.

SHAPING SEAM ALLOWANCES

Clip Inside Curves

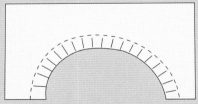

Clip the seam allowance to reduce bulk when the work is turned right side out. Get better results by clipping closer together.

Notch Outside Curves

Cut notches from the outer edge of the fabric toward the stitched seamline, stopping just a few threads inside the seamline. The notches loosen up the seam allowance so it can lie flatter when the project is turned right side out. For sharper curves, make notches closer together.

Trim Bulk from Corners

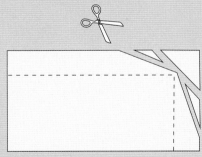

Trim excess bulk from seam allowance corners to keep fabric from bunching up when you turn it right side out. First, cut corners straight across, a few threads away from the corner stitching. Remove a bit more from the sides of the cut if the fabric is thick.

My Sewing Necessities

I'll repeat the old saw—the right tool for the right project can make all the difference! These are my most-loved, top-performing products that make sewing and crafting an absolute pleasure.

See Resources (page 143) for information about where to order products.

SEWING MACHINE AND ACCESSORIES

- A ¼″ foot keeps your seams accurate.

- A walking foot keeps layers of batting and fabric in place while you sew.

- A regular household iron is just fine for the projects in this book.

FUSIBLES

- Paper-backed fusible webbing, such as HeatnBond Lite, holds two fabrics together.

- Double-sided fusibles without paper backing, such as Wonder-Web or fast2fuse MEDIUM fusible interfacing, are easy to sew through yet stiffen fabrics nicely.

- Heavyweight paper-backed fusibles, such as HeatnBond Ultrahold, are useful when you need the bonded fabric to be really crisp.

- Double-sided heavyweight fusible interfacing, such as fast2fuse HEAVY by C&T Publishing or Craf-Tex Plus by Bosal, is very stiff yet sewable.

- Fusible grid makes it easy to sew perfect patchwork, and adds a layer of interfacing. I use Pellon 820 Quilter's Grid for a rigid interfacing and Bosal Quilting and Craft Grid for a softer finish. Bosal's 2½″ Fusible Grid is great for using with 2½″ precut strip bundles.

- Fusible fleece or fusible batting adds washable, durable padding with the ease of fusibility. Pellon's 987F Fusible Fleece is slightly thicker than Bosal's 325 Fusible Batting.

- Spray baste is a special aerosol glue designed to temporarily hold layers of fabric together. Usually sold to quilters, it can be found in quilt shops and craft stores.

SCISSORS

- Sewing scissors with spring grips help keep your hands from getting tired.

- Thread snips with spring grips are also easy on your hands.

- Pinking shears are great for adding a decorative edge or to keep cotton fabric from fraying.

- Craft scissors are simply inexpensive scissors that you don't plan to use for cutting fabric.

THREAD

- Extra-strong thread. My all-time favorite is Gütermann Extra Strong thread. It is an essential when you are gathering tightly and putting a lot of tension on your thread.

- Sewing machine thread. I use Aurifil Mako 50-weight. It's thin, strong, and sinks into fabric when used for piecing.

- Variegated thread, such as the gorgeous variations in the Aurifil line, add a decorative effect.

NOTIONS

- **Seam rippers** are essential for unsewing (page 12) or cutting a small slit in the fabric. Alex Anderson's 4-in-1 Essential Sewing Tool is best.

- **Doll needles**. These are fantastic for passing thread through something reaaaalllly thick, such as when tufting a pillow.

- **Flathead pins** are easy to grab. Get the kind that won't melt if you iron over them, like Dritz Flat Flower Head Pins.

- **Fray Check**, a seam sealant applied by the drop, made by Dritz. It keeps fabric from unraveling, knots from undoing, and seams from breaking.

- **Fabric markers with disappearing ink** make it easy to trace the templates on the fabric without worrying about removing the marks. FriXion pen marks come off with the heat of an iron.

- **Marking rulers**. I used fast2mark 6″ and 18″ Quilter's Rulers. The beveled edges make it possible for you to use a fine-tip marker and trace templates right on top of the pattern lines.

- **Rotary cutter, ruler, and mat**. I like the Olfa brand. The yellow lines are easy to see. Olfa also makes a cutter with an automatically retractable blade.

- **Nonstick ironing or gluing sheet**. I use Silicone Release Paper by C&T, a great nonstick surface for hot gluing and ironing with fusibles.

- **Gridded design wall flannel by Kaffe Fassett**. Utterly perfect for planning all of your projects—the gray is a perfect neutral that won't compete with or distract from any fabrics you're using. Fabric pieces stick and are easy to rearrange, so you can step back and look at your designs from a distance. The grid is a practical 2″ square; it keeps all your layouts straight!

- **Polyester fiberfill**. It's sold in bags by weight at most craft stores. You can usually find two grades. Basic polyfill is coarser and better for large projects. Premium or supreme polyfill is better for smaller projects because it's made of finer strands that are easier to compact into small spaces and resist clumping.

- **Freezer paper** is sold by the roll near aluminum foil and plastic wrap in grocery stores. Use it for making patterns, appliquéing projects, and stabilizing fabric run through your home printer.

- **Transparent template plastic** for tracing the patterns listed on the pullout pages. Plastic pattern pieces can be used over and over and are much easier to trace than their paper counterparts. If you're in a pinch, you can use a clear or frosted folder from an office supply store, or my favorite—flexible plastic kitchen cutting boards from the dollar store!

- **Turning tool**. This thin, blunt instrument is used for smoothing out curved seams and pushing out corners in sewn projects. A chopstick or blunt pencil will work, too.

- **Glues:**

  FABRIC GLUE. Designed for fabric, this glue remains flexible when dry and is laundry proof.

  WHITE GLUE. Regular Elmer's-type glue. Avoid using the "school" type (washable) glue, which is less permanent. (It gets sticky in humid weather.)

  GLUESTICK. A special fabric gluestick is perfect for these projects, but a regular old washable gluestick is just fine.

  HOT-GLUE GUN. Perfect for quickly and permanently gluing fabric pieces in place.

- **Buttons**. While beautiful buttons are available at sewing and craft stores these days, why not raid grandma's button box or repurpose buttons from a vintage garment?

Brit Boutique from Carnaby Street by Pat Bravo
for Art Gallery Fabrics

For the Living Area

Our space speaks about who we are. Decorate *your* environment with original, fun projects made by *you*. Customize projects in your favorite colorway to match your home.

Each one is its own conversation starter. These projects will be the first thing your guest will see and the last thing they'll forget.

Harlequin Star Pillow Chair

FINISHED SIZE: 46″ diameter × 23⅓″ high

For the star pillow, I was inspired by a Victorian pincushion I saw in a museum years ago. What could make that more fun? Blowing up the size about 100 times and exaggerating the diamond effect with patchwork using Kaffe Fassett Collective fabrics by Westminster! Star pillows are so much fun to make—it's almost magical to see how flat panels come together to make something so over-the-top three-dimensional.

No one can resist a star pillow; make one and see!

CONSTRUCTION OVERVIEW: Iron fabric squares to a fusible grid to make Nine-Patch panels. (The grid reinforces the fabric and makes perfect seams a snap!) Back with muslin for further reinforcement. Join five to make the top of the star, another five for the bottom of the star, and five more for the side panels. Join the top to the side panels, and then the bottom to the top/side assembly. Turn right side out, stuff, and tuft the center with buttons.

Materials Requirements and Cutting Instructions

Harlequin Star Pillow Chair

FABRIC	FOR	CUTTING
4 yards assorted coordinating fabrics	Patchwork panels	Cut 135 squares 6″ × 6″.
4⅛ yards muslin	Reinforcement panels	Cut 15 squares 16½″ × 16½″.
4½ yards fusible 1″ grid (I used 1″ Fusible Quilter's Grid, which comes on a 45″-wide roll.)	Patchwork base	Cut 15 panels 18″ × 18″.

FINDINGS: Extra-strong thread such as Gütermann Extra Strong Thread, 10-lb. bag basic polyester fiberfill, 2 shank buttons 1″ wide, nonstick ironing sheet or a piece of white paper, spray baste

TOOLS: Sewing machine with walking foot, extra-long needle such as a doll needle, turning tool

For more information about the supplies needed for this project, see My Sewing Necessities (page 14). For information about where to buy materials, see Resources (page 143).

The Harlequin Star Pillow Chair can be thrown on the floor like an ottoman or placed on a sofa for extra-comfy seating.

Getting It Together

All seams are ⅜″.

NINE-PATCH SQUARES

1. Work with the fusible (rough) side of a fusible grid square facing up. Place 9 fabric squares faceup on top of the grid, using the gridlines as a guide.

Technical marvel

Since you will be sewing on the grid and not the fabric, small discrepancies will not show in the finished product.

Fuse fabric to grid.

Begin by arranging squares on fusible grid.

2. Cover the grid with a sheet of white paper or nonstick ironing sheet. Use an iron set according to the fusible instructions to gently fuse the squares onto the fusible grid. Remove the paper/ironing sheet and give the pieces an extra press from the iron to ensure that all fabric squares are firmly attached.

3. At each vertical seam, fold the grid inward (fabric sides together) along the seamline and finger-press seams in the grid. Sew along each seam, backstitching at the beginning and end of the seam, to enclose the edges of the fabric. Slit the seams open with narrow, sharp scissors. Press all seams open.

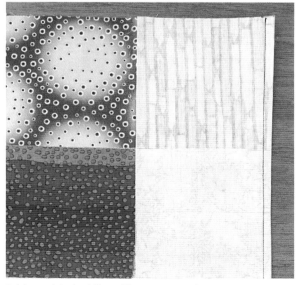

Fold on printed gridlines. Finger-press and sew.

4. Repeat Step 3 for all horizontal seams. Pause to admire your crisp, perfect seams! Figure A

5. Repeat Steps 1–4 to make 15 patchwork squares.

6. Spray-baste 16½″ reinforcement muslin squares to the back of each Nine-Patch square. From now on, treat the muslin/patchwork unit as a single panel.

7. On the wrong side of all patchwork squares, mark a dot on each corner ⅜″ from each edge. These dots will serve as guides for where to start and stop stitching during the star panel assembly.

A. Seams sewn and corners marked

STAR ASSEMBLY

1. Set your machine to a short stitch length (2.0) to prevent the fiberfill from escaping later. Sew 5 patchwork squares together with all intersections radiating out from the same point, pinning intersections and stitching between the dots. Start sewing from the outside edge to the center of the star shape, folding all previously sewn seam allowances out of the way. Backstitch at the beginning and end of each seam. Figure B

2. Sew another 5 sections together in the same manner. Now you have completed the top and the bottom of the pillow. Press all seam allowances open. Figure C

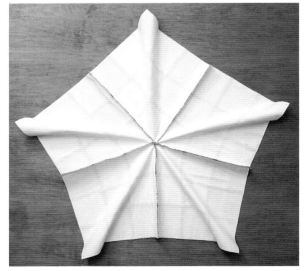

B. Sew from outside toward center of star.

C. Top of star

PILLOW ASSEMBLY

The five remaining Nine-Patch/muslin squares will serve as the side panels between the star halves.

1. Pin 2 adjoining sides of a side-panel square to 2 raw edges, which form a star panel "point," right sides together. Sew together, 1 side of the point at a time, stitching between the marked dots and folding previously sewn seam allowances out of the way as you sew. Backstitch at the beginning and end of seams.

2. Repeat Step 1 to sew the remaining 4 squares, which form the other points of the star panel.

Sew the side squares between the star panel points.

3. Use the method described in Steps 1 and 2 to attach the other star panel to the remaining sides of the side-panel squares. On the last seam, leave a 4″ section open for turning and stuffing.

4. Turn the star right side out through the opening. Push the corners out with a turning tool. Press all seam edges.

5. Stuff the star firmly with fiberfill, making sure to get fiberfill into all points of the star. For a smooth result when stuffing such a large project, first stuff the corners, then a little of each section, moving around the star several times before finishing.

6. Ladder stitch (page 12) the opening closed with matching thread.

7. To button-tuft the star, thread an extra-long needle with 2 strands 60″ long of extra-strong thread. Tie the thread ends securely to a button. Run through the pillow from a star center to the other star center. Loop through the second button and bring the needle back through the thickness of the pillow. Loop through the first button and repeat. To finish, tie a surgeon's knot (page 13) under the first button. Clip threads and hide ends under the button.

Tufting the star gives it added dimension.

Biscornu Pillow

FINISHED SIZE: 15″ diameter × 7″ high

The French call this shape a *biscornu*, which literally means "multiple points." It also means "that which is quirky, irregular, skewed, and bizarre." I like that. I like that a lot. …

I was experimenting with this shape and discovered the secondary zigzag design when I used pieced panels. Bonus!

For this project I used Kaffe Fassett Collective fabrics by Westminster, A Closer Look by La Todera for Clothworks, and a few other scraps from my stash.

CONSTRUCTION OVERVIEW: Stitch-and-flip patchwork strips form four panels that form a secondary zigzag pattern when offset and stitched together. Stuff and tuft with buttons.

Materials Requirements and Cutting Instructions

Biscornu Pillow

FABRIC	FOR	CUTTING
⅜ yard each of 5 coordinating fabrics (Fabrics A–E) or 4 precut 2½″-strip bundles, each containing at least 40 strips. Divide the bundles into 5 color groups.		
Fabric A (red ombré) and Fabric E (black and white) ⅜ yard each or 4 strips 2½″ wide	Pillow	From each fabric, cut 4 strips 2½″ × width of fabric. Subcut into 4 pieces 2½″ × 20½″ and 4 pieces 2½″ × 4½″.
Fabric B (turquoise) and Fabric D (black cats)	Pillow	From each fabric, cut 3 strips 2½″ × width of fabric. Subcut into 4 pieces 2½″ × 16½″ and 4 pieces 2½″ × 8½″.
Fabric C (mirage stripe)	Pillow	Cut 3 strips 2½″ × width of fabric. Subcut into 8 pieces 2½″ × 12½″.
⅝ yard muslin or scrap fabric, starched and ironed	Reinforcement	Cut 2 squares 20″ × 20″. Subcut each diagonally twice to yield 4 triangles each, 8 total.

FINDINGS: 20-oz. bag basic polyester fiberfill, 2 large (at least 1″) buttons, extra-strong polyester thread in a color that matches the buttons

TOOLS: Sewing machine, disappearing-ink fabric marker or pencil, turning tool, gluestick

For more information about the supplies needed for this project, see My Sewing Necessities (page 14). For information about where to buy materials, see Resources (page 143).

Brighten up your sofa or a special chair with the unusual Biscornu Pillow.

Getting It Together

SIDE A TRIANGLES

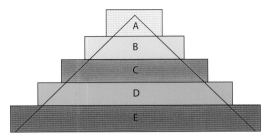

Side A triangle: Make 4.

1. Center a Fabric A 20½″ strip along the base of a muslin base triangle, right side up, aligning raw edges. Pin or glue this first strip in place with a gluestick.

Center the first strip against the base of the triangle.

Tip

To center strips, finger-press the triangle and the strip. Match creases.

2. Center a Fabric B 16″ strip on top of the first strip, right side down, aligning raw edges. Make sure the top corners overhang the muslin base on both sides. Sew through all layers with a ¼″ seam on the top edge.

Sew second strip to first strip.

3. Flip over the Fabric B strip and press.

Flip up the second strip.

4. Repeat Steps 2 and 3 with a Fabric C 12″ strip, a Fabric D 8″ strip, and a Fabric E 4″ strip to completely cover the base fabric. Press.

5. Turn over the triangle. With a rotary cutter, cut the strips flush with the sides of the muslin triangle.

Trim excess strip fabric from the base fabric.

6. Secure the small triangle of Fabric E to the base muslin with basting or a bit of glue.

Use a gluestick to fasten the loose top corner flaps to the base fabric.

7. Repeat Steps 1–6 to make 3 more Side A triangles.

SIDE B TRIANGLES

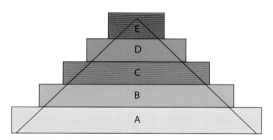

Side B triangle: Make 4.

Repeat Steps 1–6 from the Side A Triangles instructions (page 27), using the remaining 4 muslin triangles as base fabric. Use the following sewing order:

- Fabric E
- Fabric D
- Fabric C
- Fabric B
- Fabric A

PILLOW ASSEMBLY

Note: Use a ½″ seam allowance for all Pillow Assembly seams.

1. Sew the short sides of 2 Side A triangles together, pinning each intersection where stripes meet. Join with a ½″ seam. Press seams open. Repeat with the 2 remaining Side A triangles.

2. Join the pieced triangle units together with a ½″ seam, pinning the intersection. Press seams open.

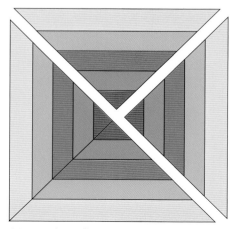

Join triangles to form a square.

3. Use the method from Steps 1 and 2 to sew the Side B triangles together to form a square.

4. On the wrong side of the large squares, mark the corners with dots ½″ from the adjacent edges. Mark the sides of the squares at their midpoints (fold in half to find) with a dot ½″ from the edge. Clip the seams ¼″ in at the midpoint marks as shown.

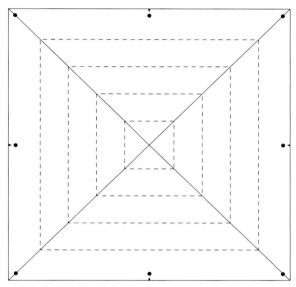

Mark and clip center of each side of both squares.

5. Place panels A and B right sides together, matching the corners of each square to the midpoints of the other square. After you pin all 8 corners to the midpoints, match the edges and add additional pins to the straight seams.

Match the corners of each square with the midpoints of the other square.

6. Sew together with a ½″ seam, leaving a 4″ section on a straight edge unsewn. Clip the corners and press the seams open.

7. Turn the pillow through the opening, making sure to push out all corners.

8. Stuff with polyester fiberfill, adding small bits to the corners to fill them out completely.

9. Ladder stitch (page 12) the opening closed.

10. Tuft with buttons (see Pillow Assembly, Step 7, for the Harlequin Star Pillow Chair, page 23).

Tip

Wax your thread (use quilter's beeswax or rub the thread on a candle) before you use it to secure the buttons. The waxed thread has a better grip, so it will help you make a better indentation.

Tufting makes the side zigzag illusion more pronounced.

Malaysian Mini Mat

FINISHED SIZE: 10″ × 10″

It's said that a larger version of these rugs, crafted from available scraps, is used widely as a kitchen rug in Malaysia.

I saw one online, and it was love at first sight. I was determined to figure out how they were made. It wasn't until a friend gifted me one that I was able to disassemble it to discover how the folded units were crafted.

Funny that during my research I found out that the Amish have their own version of kitchen rugs called *Staubfänger* ("dust catchers"), also made from folded scraps. What a small world we live in!

Try your hand at this mini version. If you catch the bug, try making your own kitchen rug for in front of your sink!

For this project, I used Kaffe Fassett striped fabrics by Rowan; Marcia Derse fabrics by Windham; and striped, repurposed fabrics from my stash.

CONSTRUCTION OVERVIEW: Press fabric rectangles into units. Draw a grid on base fabric. Arrange rings of folded fabric units. Pin and sew. Cover the remaining raw fabric edges in the center with a padded fabric square.

Materials Requirements and Cutting Instructions

Malaysian Mini Mat

FABRIC	FOR	CUTTING
Fabric scraps or yardage to total ⅞ yard	Outer row (¾ yard)	Cut 32 rectangles 4″ × 6″.
	Middle row (⅝ yard)	Cut 24 rectangles 4″ × 6″.
	Inner row (½ yard)	Cut 16 rectangles 4″ × 6″.
	Center puff	Cut 2 squares 4″ × 4″.
⅓ yard or fat quarter muslin	Base	Cut 1 square 10″ × 10″.
⅓ yard or 10″ square section of prepackaged 1″ fusible grid	Base	Cut 1 square 10″ × 10″.
11″ square felt	Backing	Cut 1 square 8½″ × 8½″. Finish edges with pinking shears.

FINDINGS: Scrap of polyester fiberfill or batting to fill 4″ square, coordinating thread

TOOLS: Sewing machine with walking foot; clear template plastic; fabric glue; rotary cutter, ruler, and mat

Find Malaysian Mini Mat Corner Marking Pattern on pullout page P2). Trace onto clear template plastic and cut out to create the corner marking template.

For more information about the supplies needed for this project, see My Sewing Necessities (page 14). For information about where to buy materials, see Resources (page 143).

Use the Malaysian Mini Mat under a vase or mug.

Getting It Together

FOLDED UNITS

1. Fold 4″ × 6″ rectangles in half lengthwise. Press.

Fold 4″ × 6″ rectangles in half.

2. Fold the short ends on the diagonal so the raw edges from the diagonal fold align with the raw edges of the strip. Press.

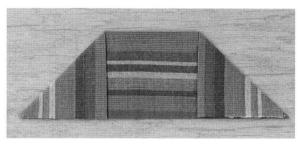

Fold short ends on the diagonal.

3. Fold the strip in half widthwise, folded corners to the inside, matching raw edges and points. Press.

Press in half widthwise.

4. Fold the diagonal ends back, beginning at the start of the angle, keeping raw edges aligned. Press.

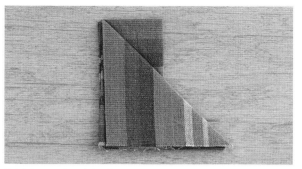

Fold diagonal ends back.

Tip

If using striped fabric, cut units with stripes running lengthwise.

PREPARE BASE

1. Fuse the 10″ square of fusible grid onto the 10″ muslin square. Tada! A premarked base!

2. Mark the grid into concentric squares as shown in the base grid diagram. Use the corner marking template to draw rounded corners onto the grid with a marker.

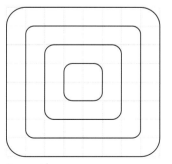

Base grid

APPLY FABRIC UNITS

1. Follow the outer row placement diagram (below) to arrange folded units onto the base fabric. Start on the center of the top edge. Place a unit with raw edges touching the outermost drawn line and triangle edges pointing to the right. Place a second unit 1 grid square to the right.

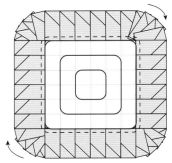

Outer row placement

2. Tuck both triangle edges from the first unit inside the triangle edges of the second unit. Each unit has space to unfold and accommodate the neighboring unit. Pin in place. Repeat with the remainder of the outer row, following the diagram and placing the units in a clockwise direction.

Tip

To make a smooth curve on each corner, use three units at every corner. Take your time arranging curves. Make sure the corners of each unit are tucked inside the corners of the next one, as described in Step 2.

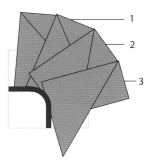

3. Using a sewing machine with a walking foot and coordinating thread, sew units to the base fabric ¼″ from the raw edges, removing pins as you sew.

Tip

To make it easier to fit the work under the walking foot, locate the presser foot pressure adjustment dial on your sewing machine. Adjust the dial to allow maximum lift of the presser foot. Once the foot is positioned, increase pressure again. Loosen pressure to remove work from the machine.

4. Use the same process to add the center row of strips to the base fabric, following the center row placement diagram.

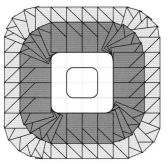

Center row placement

5. Add the inner row of strips, following the inner row placement diagram.

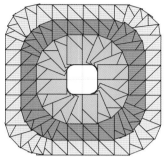

Inner row placement

CENTER PUFF

1. Sew the 4″ center squares right sides together with a ¼″ seam. Clip corners. Clip a 1″ slit in the center of 1 side and turn right side out. Push out the corners. Press the edges. Stuff lightly with fiberfill or a square scrap of batting.

2. Pin in place over the center of the mat, slit side down. Topstitch ⅛″ from the edge with matching thread.

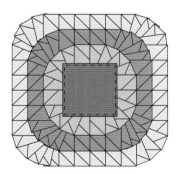

BACK OF MAT

1. Flip the mat over and trim the base fabric ¼″ beyond the outermost row of stitching.

2. Apply fabric glue liberally to the back of the felt backing square. Center the square on the back of the mat, covering raw edges of the base fabric. Place the mat right side up and weight with a book until the glue is dry.

3. To reinforce any area where the base fabric might show through on the right side of the mat, use a bit of fabric glue to secure layers of fabric tabs together.

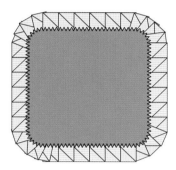

Folded Wall Flowers

FINISHED SIZES: Large: 16″ diameter; Medium: 13″; Small: 10″

Populate your blank walls with fabric flowers! (Think of your walls as empty fields.) These flowers whip up in a jiffy with your favorite quilting fabric, fusible webbing, and a few clever folds. You will quickly realize that you can make them *any* size just by varying the size of the circle template.

For this project, I used the Carnaby Street collection by Pat Bravo for Art Gallery Fabrics and A Closer Look collection by La Todera for Clothworks.

CONSTRUCTION OVERVIEW: Fuse two of your favorite fabrics into circle units. Fold and join into a multi-unit origami flower to grace your walls alone or in a group!

Materials Requirements and Cutting Instructions

Folded Wall Flowers

FABRIC	FOR	CUTTING
¾ yard print (Fabric 1). Allow extra if you want to fussy cut large motifs.	Large flower Outer and inner petals	Cut 8 squares 9″ × 9″.
½ yard coordinating print (Fabric 2)	Large flower Half of 2-color petals	Cut 4 squares 9″ × 9″.
½ yard coordinating print (Fabric 3)	Large flower Half of 2-color petals	Cut 4 squares 9″ × 9″.
1½ yards double-sided fusible webbing (I used Wonder-Web.)	Large flower Interfacing	Cut 8 squares 9″ × 9″.
⅝ yard print (Fabric 1)	Medium flower Outer and inner petals	Cut 8 squares 7½″ × 7½″.
⅜ yard coordinating print (Fabric 2)	Medium flower Half of 2-color petals	Cut 4 squares 7½″ × 7½″.
⅜ yard coordinating print (Fabric 3)	Medium flower Half of 2-color petals	Cut 4 squares 7½″ × 7½″.
1 yard double-sided fusible webbing	Medium flower Interfacing	Cut 8 squares 7½″ × 7½″.
½ yard print (Fabric 1)	Small flower Outer and inner petals	Cut 8 squares 6″ × 6″.
⅜ yard coordinating print (Fabric 2)	Small flower Half of 2-color petals	Cut 4 squares 6″ × 6″.
⅜ yard coordinating print (Fabric 3)	Small flower Half of 2-color petals	Cut 4 squares 6″ × 6″.
¾ yard double-sided fusible webbing	Small flower Interfacing	Cut 8 squares 6″ × 6″.

FINDINGS: Buttons, yo-yos, pompons, or other embellishment for the flower center; 6″ length of extra-strong thread for hanger; coordinating thread

TOOLS: Sewing machine, clear template plastic, iron, pinking shears, turning tool, hot-glue gun and sticks

Find Folded Wall Flowers Marking Templates A, B, and C for the size flower desired on pullout page P1. Trace onto clear template plastic and cut out to create templates A, B, and C.

For more information about the supplies needed for this project, see My Sewing Necessities (page 14). For information about where to buy materials, see Resources (page 143).

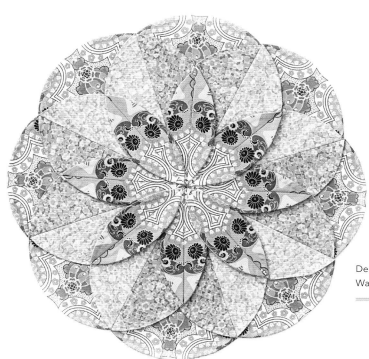

Tip

Use patterned and/or darker fabrics for this project. When the webbing melts, it darkens some light fabrics.

Decorate your walls with Folded Wall Flowers in three sizes.

Getting It Together

BASE CIRCLES

For any size of flower, follow these instructions. All seam allowances are ¼″.

1. Trace the marking template A circle onto the wrong side of each Fabric 1 square.

2. On a work surface, layer in this order:

- Fusible webbing (bottom)
- Fabric 2, faceup (middle)
- Fabric 1, facedown (top)

Pin together. Make 4 sets and set aside.

3. On a work surface, layer in this order:

- Fusible webbing (bottom)
- Fabric 3, faceup (middle)
- Fabric 1, facedown (top)

Pin together. Make 4 sets.

4. Sew completely around the traced line on all stacks.

5. Trim ¼″ from the sewn lines with pinking shears.

6. Cut a 1″ slit in the center of the Fabric 1 layers only.

7. Turn each circle unit right side out and use a turning tool to smooth curves. Press with a hot iron to fuse fabrics and seal the turning slit.

OUTER PETAL ASSEMBLY

1. With a disappearing-ink fabric marker, trace lines using marking templates B and C onto the Fabric 1 side of each fused circle. Turn each circle over and mark the same lines on the reverse, matching positions to the lines on the front.

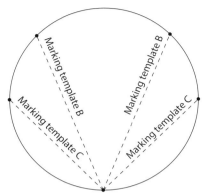

Mark fused circles with sewing lines using marking templates B and C.

2. Pair a Fabric 2 circle and a Fabric 3 circle, placing the Fabric 2 and 3 sides together and matching template B lines. Pin. Sew along 1 of the template B lines.

3. Sew 3 more pairs and then join pairs to make a complete circle by joining as in Step 2: Place Fabrics 2 and 3 sides together, matching the unsewn template B lines. Sew from the outer edge toward the bulky center. Now you have made the basic flower shape with some large, loose petals on the front. Press all seams open with a hot iron.

> ## Tip
> Sew petals together from the outside to the inside of the flower.

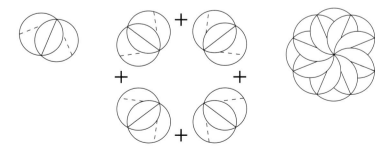

Order of sewing circles

INNER PETALS

1. With a disappearing-ink fabric marker, mark line C on the back of each loose petal you created in Outer Petal Assembly (page 40). Position the template to match the line you marked on the front of the petal in Step 1 of Outer Petal Assembly.

2. Pinch the petals together along the C lines. Sew on the line from the outside of the petal to the center of the flower. Press all pairs open with a hot iron to permanently fix the creases.

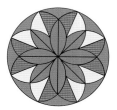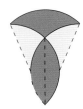

Full flower and close-up of ⅛ section of flower, with small petals sewn and pressed open

FINISHING

1. Hot-glue the embellishments of your choice to the flower's center. Try yo-yos, vintage buttons, pompons, felt flowers—you name it!

2. Turn the flower over. Hand stitch a short length of heavy thread about ¼ of the way down from the top edge of the flower. Knot the ends of the thread together 1″ from the stitch to form a hanging loop.

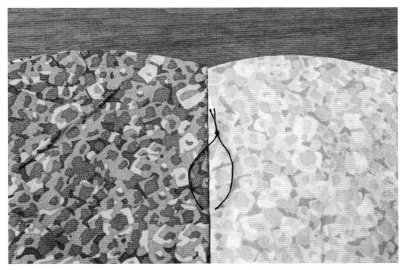

Hanging loop

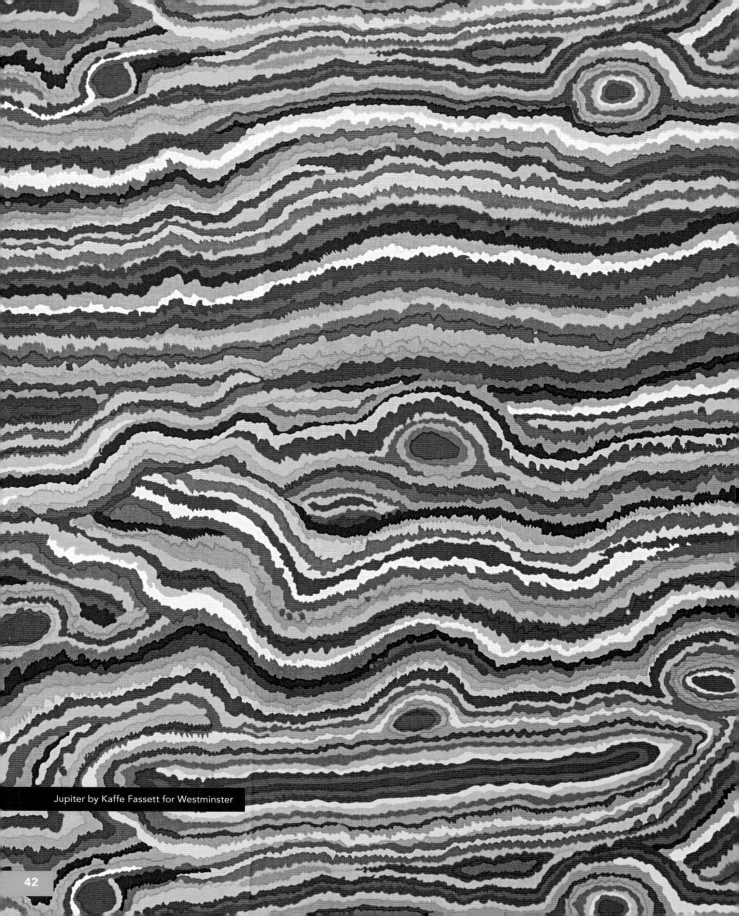

Jupiter by Kaffe Fassett for Westminster

For the Dining Area

Fabric projects are a fabulous way to add color and softness to an often hard-edged environment. Gifts for the kitchen are always welcome since they have to be renewed every so often. These projects are all practical, easy to make, and easy on the eyes.

Lily Pad Centerpiece

FINISHED SIZE: Varies with arrangement.
Large lily pads: 12˝ diameter; Medium lily pads: 9˝; Small lily pads: 6˝

This centerpiece has so many possibilities. Make it out of striped fabrics, shot cottons, or even a patchwork of different fabrics. Rearrange the layout to the shape of your table. The lily pads are not sewn together, so the possibilities for rearranging are infinite! Pull one to use as a coaster or under a flower vase. Add Water Lily Brooches (page 98) for the finishing touch.

The striped ombré fabric I used is Kim in green by Kaffe Fassett for Westminster Fabrics.

CONSTRUCTION OVERVIEW: Sew three sizes of quilted lily pads from eight wedges of striped fabric each. For my Lily Pad Centerpiece, I made two large, three medium, and five small lily pads for a centerpiece that is approximately 18˝ × 42˝.

Materials Requirements and Cutting Instructions

This project contains many bias edges, so take special care with the fabric. *Thoroughly starch and iron fabrics* before starting the project. Starching the fabric virtually eliminates stretching and makes the bias edges on wedge sections a snap to sew!

Lily Pad Centerpiece

FABRIC	FOR	CUTTING
1¼ yards stripes, ombré, shot cottons, or other fabric	Large lily pads (Makes 2.)	Cut 2 strips 6½″ × width of fabric.
		Use template L to subcut into 16 large wedges.
	Medium lily pads (Makes 3.)	Cut 3 strips 5″ × width of fabric.
		Use template M to subcut into 24 medium wedges.
	Small lily pads (Makes 5.)	Cut 3 strips 3½″ × width of fabric.
		Use template S to subcut into 40 small wedges.
1 yard linen	Backing: Large Medium Small	Cut 2 squares 14″ × 14″. Cut 3 squares 11″ × 11″. Cut 5 squares 8″ × 8″.

FINDINGS: Scraps of fusible webbing, topstitching thread in colors that coordinate with the lily pad fabric

TOOLS: Sewing machine with walking foot, clear template plastic, spray starch, turning tool

Find Lily Pad Centerpiece Patterns L, M, and S on pullout page P1. Trace onto clear template plastic, transfer alignment dots, and cut out to create templates L, M, and S.

For more information about the supplies needed for this project, see My Sewing Necessities (page 14). For information about where to buy materials, see Resources (page 143).

Tip

Cut the strips in varied order to create different stripe variations on the finished lily pads. To make lily pads like those shown, be certain to cut eight identical wedges for each lily pad to ensure that the stripes match.

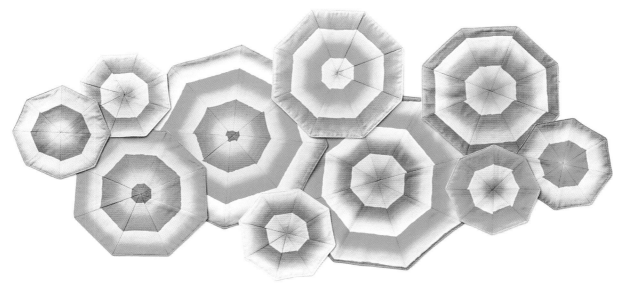

Sew lily pads in three sizes to make a centerpiece that you can rearrange to fit the shape and size of your space—and your mood! Need a coaster on the spur of the moment? Steal a small lily pad from the arrangement! Need a trivet to rest a main dish on? Pull a large lily pad! Endless combinations and uses!

Getting It Together

Use ¼″ seam allowances. To make a lily pad from any size:

1. Mark 8 wedges at the narrow end with the dot indicated on the pattern.

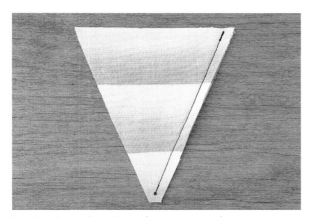

Marking dots at the bottom of wedges makes for neater seams later.

2. Sew wedges together in pairs, stopping and backstitching at the dot. Press the seams open. Make 4 paired units.

3. Pin the wedge units together in pairs, placing a pin at each end of the open seamlines. Sew together along 1 edge, stopping and backstitching at the center seam. Press the seams open. Make 2 lily pad halves.

Technical marvel

Pressing open the seams in Step 2 makes it easy to see exactly where to stop sewing in this step.

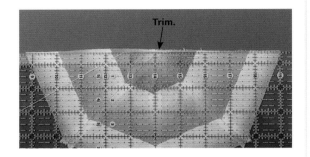

Sew the lily pad assembly to linen backing layer.

4. Pin the lily pad halves right sides together, pinning center seams together carefully. Sew. Press the seams open.

6. Using a seam ripper, carefully unsew (page 12) a 1″ opening on 1 of the seams between wedges.

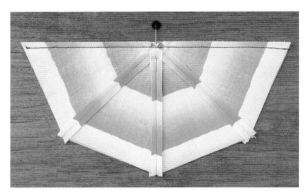

Pin center seams.

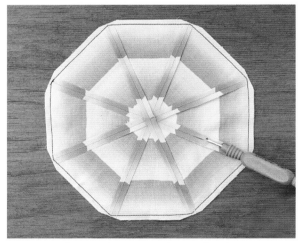

Unsew a small section between wedges to allow for turning.

5. Place the backing fabric right side up. Place a lily pad right side down in the center of the backing fabric and pin. Sew completely around the lily pad using a ¼″ seam allowance.

Trim the backing fabric even with the lily pad. Clip corners straight across.

7. Turn lily pads right side out through the new opening. Push the corners out. Press. Close the seam with a ladder stitch (page 12), using matching thread.

8. Topstitch ⅛″ from the edge of all lily pads. Trim threads.

CENTERPIECE ASSEMBLY

Arrange lily pads as you wish.

Tip

Making this for a round table? Rearrange lily pads to make a more compact, "round" layout.

Optional: Add Water Lilies

These Water Lily Brooches (page 98) are the perfect complement to the Lily Pad Centerpiece! Make several to sprinkle along your table runner.

Tip

Pin the brooches in place through one layer of fabric only so the pins don't scratch your table surface.

Plumeria Placemat

Plumerias are the simplest of flowers—just five smooth petals with a tiny center. This project came about when I was experimenting with a faux cathedral window technique made with units of four circles. Always pushing the (fabric) envelope, I had to see what would happen with five circles. *Et voilà*—a simple flower shape like the plumeria!

For this project, I used Asian Circles by Kaffe Fassett for Westminster, Purl from A Closer Look by La Todera for Clothworks, and Shot Cotton by Kaffe Fassett for Rowan.

CONSTRUCTION OVERVIEW: Sew five double-sided circular petals lined with fusible fleece. Mark and join the petals at angles. Topstitch and add tiny yo-yos in the center.

Materials Requirements and Cutting Instructions

The fabric requirements are for one placemat.

Plumeria Placemat

FABRIC	FOR	CUTTING
⅝ yard each of 2 coordinating prints	Large petal fronts and backs	Cut 5 squares 9½″ × 9½″ from each fabric.
⅛ yard solid fabric	Mini yo-yos	Cut 5 circles using template C.
⅝ yard fusible fleece, 45″ wide	Petals	Cut 5 squares 9½″ × 9½″.

FINDINGS: Thread in coordinating color for topstitching, extra-heavy thread, regular sewing thread in color to match the yo-yo fabric

TOOLS: Sewing machine with walking foot, clear template plastic, pinking shears, disappearing-ink fabric marker, turning tool, gluestick

Find Plumeria Placemat marking templates A and B, and Pattern C, on pullout page P2. Trace onto template plastic and cut out to create templates A, B, and C.

For more information about the supplies needed for this project, see My Sewing Necessities (page 14). For information about where to buy materials, see Resources (page 143).

The Plumeria Placemat is easy to make with a few seams and folds. Highlight your table with these placemats that won't be like anyone else's!

Getting It Together

FLOWER PETALS

1. Trace template A on the wrong side of each petal front fabric piece.

2. Make 5 stacks in the following order:

- Fusible fleece, fusible side down

- Petal back fabric, right side up

- Petal front fabric, right side down

Pin each stack in the center.

3. Using a walking foot, sew around the circle on top of the marked line. Trim with pinking shears ¼″ from the stitching.

4. Place template B on top of the petal front fabric of the sewn stack, matching the top curved edge with the curved sewing line. Trace straight edges with a fabric marker.

5. Carefully cut a 1″ slit in the top layer, petal front fabric only, between 1 of the drawn lines and the stitching.

6. Turn right side out, using a turning tool to smooth the curves. Pinch the edges of the turning slit together. Fuse the fabric layer to fusible fleece with a hot iron.

7. Using a fabric marker and template B, trace the straight edges drawn in Step 4 onto the right side of the petal front fabric.

8. Repeat Steps 3–7 with the remaining stacks to make 5 petals.

FLOWER ASSEMBLY

1. Pair 2 petals, petal back fabrics together, matching edges and traced lines. Match and pin a set of traced lines as carefully as possible. Sew along the pinned line through all layers.

Turning slit, strategically placed

Sew 2 petals together. The folded flaps not only hide the turning slits but also create a secondary petal design—just like a real plumeria!

2. Sew the remaining 3 circles to the unit from Step 1, sewing from the outside edge toward the bulky center. Sew the first circle to the last. Fold excess layers out of your way as you sew.

Sew the remaining 3 circles to the first 2; then sew the first circle to the last.

3. Press the center petals open. Pin the petal flaps to the main petals to hold in place for topstitching in Step 4.

4. With coordinating thread, carefully topstitch ¼˝ from all edges in a continuous line.

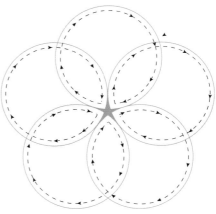

Topstitching

FLOWER CENTER

1. Using a needle threaded with a single strand of extra-heavy thread, fold over the edge of a solid-fabric circle cut from template C as you stitch ⅛″ from the edge all the way around. Use an ⅛″ stitch length, ending on the right side of the fabric.

Sew a gathering stitch around the circle.

2. Gather the circle up tightly to completely close the opening. Take a tiny backstitch between the folds. Knot the thread and bring it through to the back before trimming.

3. Repeat Steps 1 and 2 with the remaining 4 solid-fabric circles to make 5 mini yo-yos.

4. Overlap the mini yo-yos in the center of the placemat, securing each with a dab from a glue stick.

5. Using thread to match the yo-yos, whipstitch (page 12) the outer edges of the yo-yos to the placemat petals with tiny stitches. Also stitch the yo-yos together where they touch in the center of the flower. Leave the spots where the yo-yos overlap unsewn to add dimension.

Done! Now set the table and have a victory snack!

Secure yo-yos with gluestick to hold in place while you sew.

Peep Show Hexies Coaster Set

FINISHED SIZE: 6″ diameter

Shows off a feature fabric! Big enough to rest a mug on!

For this project, I used Deer and Mushrooms by Kokka Co., Ltd., and Jupiter by Kaffe Fassett for Westminster.

CONSTRUCTION OVERVIEW: Über simple to make—only two stitching lines! Made from six folded polygons, two hexagons, and a section of fusible web. The fusible web creates an extra moisture barrier.

Peep Show Hexies Coasters are so easy to make! Sew up a set for your own home and as quick gifts for your friends and family.

Materials Requirements and Cutting Instructions

Yardages are for six coasters.

Peep Show Hexies Coaster Set

FABRIC	FOR	CUTTING
¼ yard or more, depending on repeat, feature fabric	Fussy-cut hexagons (Center the feature design inside the template before cutting.)	Cut 6 hexagons using template A.
½ yard coordinating print	Backing	Cut 6 hexagons using template A.
½ yard coordinating print	Border hexagons	Cut 36 pieces using template B.
½ yard fusible web from 22″ roll	Fusible web	Cut 6 pieces using template A.

FINDINGS: Coordinating thread for topstitching

TOOLS: Sewing machine with walking foot, clear template plastic, Fray Check

Find Peep Show Hexies Patterns A and B on pullout page P2. Trace onto clear template plastic and cut out to create templates A and B.

For more information about the supplies needed for this project, see My Sewing Necessities (pages 14). For information about where to buy materials, see Resources (page 143).

These coasters feature I Love Cat by Lecien and Rain Cloud Ripple and Blue Moon Ripple from the Mosaic Collection by Marcia Derse for Windham.

These fabrics are from my personal collection of shirt stripes and Hoodie's Collection for Blank Quilting.

These fabrics are from my own collection of shirt stripes and Just My Type by Patty Young for Michael Miller.

Getting It Together

1. Press all skinny border template B hexagons in half lengthwise.

2. Place a fussy-cut hexagon right side down on a work surface. Top with a fusible web hexagon and a backing hexagon, right side up.

3. Following the border placement order diagram (below) and matching raw edges, pin a folded border hexagon to the backing side of the hexagon stack.

4. Place a second border hexagon, overlapping the first. Pin. Place the remaining border hexagons in the same manner (counterclockwise), pinning each to the coaster body. When you position the last folded hexagon, unpin the first enough to slip the end of the last hexagon under it. Repin.

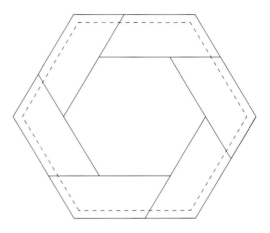

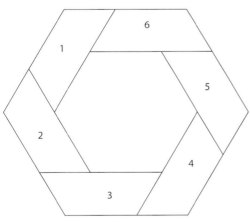

Border placement order

5. Sew around the raw edges of the hexagon unit with a ¼″ seam.

Tip

Use the walking foot on your machine. It will help keep all of the fabric layers from shifting.

6. Clip the corners straight across. Apply Fray Check to the corner stitches.

7. Flip the borders to the right side, framing the fussy-cut fabric. Push out the corners with a turning tool. Press to fuse.

8. Topstitch ¼″ from the edge of each coaster.

9. Repeat Steps 1–8 to make 5 more coasters.

Done. Now have a drink!

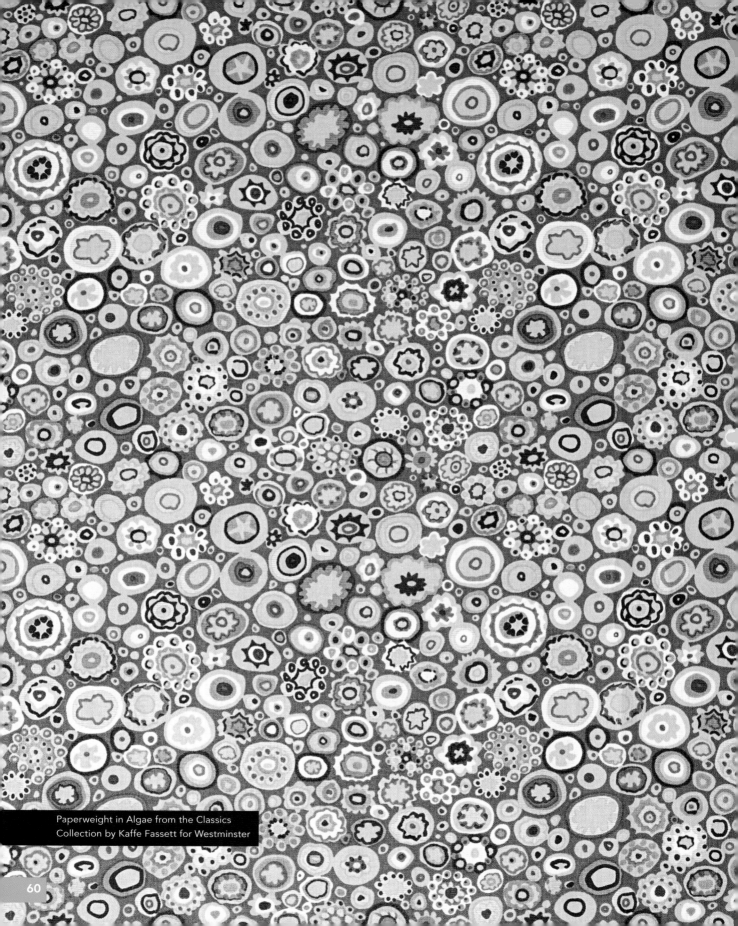

Paperweight in Algae from the Classics
Collection by Kaffe Fassett for Westminster

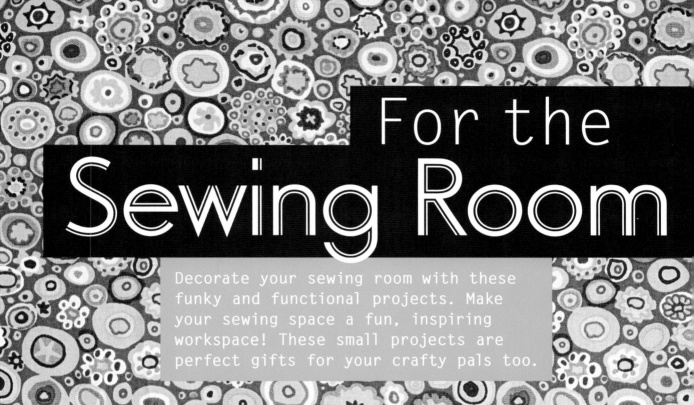

For the
Sewing Room

Decorate your sewing room with these funky and functional projects. Make your sewing space a fun, inspiring workspace! These small projects are perfect gifts for your crafty pals too.

Peacock Pincushion

FINISHED SIZE: 9″ wide × 5″ high × 4″ deep

Peacocks, fascinating peacocks. The adoration started young. My grandparents' house was next to the Madison, Wisconsin, zoo. And boy, are peacocks loud. Even when we were in the kitchen, we could hear them yelping! My favorite story was how a peacock made a break from the zoo and hid out in my grandparents' garage. I was always secretly waiting for that one to come back and visit…

Don't live next to a zoo? Make your own peacock! (And this one is quieter!)

I used some exciting fabrics in this pincushion—Paperweight in Algae by Kaffe Fassett for Westminster and Shagreen and Air Dots by La Todera for Clothworks.

CONSTRUCTION OVERVIEW: Make elongated double-sided fabric cones. Stuff and arrange them to form the peacock's famous fan tail. Add the body, turning the cone point down for a beak. Add chubby cone embellishments to the tips of the peacock fan and decorative pins to the head.

Materials Requirements and Cutting Instructions

Peacock Pincushion

FABRIC	FOR	CUTTING
⅓ yard print	Fan	Cut 6 pieces using template A.
6″ × 10″ scrap or ¼ yard print	Body	Cut 1 piece using template A.
¼ yard print	Fan accents	Cut 6 pieces using template B.
2″ × 2″ square felt	Base	Cut 1 piece using template C.

FINDINGS: Regular coordinating threads for sewing, extra-strong thread for assembly, 3 decorative straight pins for head "feathers," white glue, 3–4 oz. premium polyester fiberfill

TOOLS: Sewing machine, clear template plastic, disappearing-ink fabric marker, hot-glue gun and sticks, pinking shears

Find Peacock Pincushion Patterns A, B, and C on pullout page P2. Trace onto template plastic and cut out to create templates A, B, and C.

For more information about the supplies needed for this project, see My Sewing Necessities (page 14). For information about where to buy materials, see Resources (page 143).

The Peacock Pincushion looks complicated but is made with easy-to-sew fabric cones. It is guaranteed to brighten any sewing room.

Getting It Together

1. Fold a shape cut from pattern A in half, right sides together, matching the straight cut edges. Pin. Sew a ¼″ seam along the straight cut edges, back-stitching at the beginning and end of the seams. Trim the bulk from corners (page 13).

2. Fold a unit from Step 1 in half, matching the folded edge with the *seamline*, not with the cut edge. Finger-press. Stitch directly on top of this pressed line, backstitching at the beginning and end of the seam.

Mark the wedges neatly and sew on the pressed line. Trim the corner bulk. Press.

3. Flip the unseamed section of fabric over the seamed section to form a slim 2-layered fabric cone, right side out. Push out the point with a turning tool. Repeat Steps 1–3 for all pattern A shapes.

Flip the long cones right side out.

4. Fold the pattern B circles in half, right sides together. Finger-press. Fold the circles again (into quarters), matching creases and raw edges. Finger-press. Open the last fold. You will have half-circles with a bisecting crease.

5. Using regular thread to match the fabric and a short stitch length (2.0), sew along the creased lines of all the folded half-circles, backstitching at the beginning and end of each line. Cut the threads and trim.

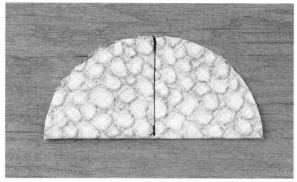

Mark circles neatly and stitch.

6. Invert half a circle over the other half to form 2-layer fabric cones, right side out.

Invert one side over the other to form double-walled cones.

7. Use the following method to stuff the cones:

- Thread a needle with at least 12″ of extra-strong thread. Take a backstitch (page 12), then stitch through both layers of fabric around the perimeter of the cone with a ¼″ stitch, ⅛″ from raw edge.

- Draw the thread up slightly and stuff the cone firmly with polyfill. Stuff each cone very firmly—think the firmness of a grape!

- Draw up the thread to close the opening completely. Backstitch, knot, and trim the thread.

8. Place the 6 long fan cones side by side. Turn all seams to the right. Thread a needle with about 24″ of extra-strong thread. Pass the needle through each cone, ⅛″ from the tip. Tie the ends of the thread together in a surgeon's knot. Bury the ends of the thread. See Construction Techniques (page 12).

On the inner part of the far left cone, attach thread on the seam with a knot, about 1″ down from the top of the cone. Run a needle through the 4 adjacent cones, 1″ from the top of the cones. Take a small stitch on the seam of the last cone in the same position. Pull the thread tight. Knot and trim the thread.

Stuffed and gathered cones

Join cones to create the peacock's famous fan. Pull the cones together before you knot the thread.

9. To form the beak, fold the tip of the body cone down about ½″, centering the seam. Pin. With matching thread, stitch the tip of the beak in place with a few tiny stitches. Bury the thread.

Audition decorative straight pins on the head of the peacock. Remove the pins 1 at a time and apply a bit of white glue to the pin shaft. Replace the pin.

Use your funkiest head pins to adorn your peacock's crown.

10. Stand the fan up on a work surface. Place the peacock body in front of the fan. Cup the fan slightly around the body. Note the points where the body touches the fan. Remove the body and apply points of hot glue to these points. Replace the body in position, holding the fan cupped around the body until the glue cools completely.

11. Glue the fan accent cones onto the tips of the fan "feathers."

12. Glue a circle of felt to the bottom of the peacock body to cover the raw edges of fabric.

A pinked felt circle will cover the peacock's naked hiney parts.

Strut your new Peacock Pincushion!

Ladybug Pincushion

FINISHED SIZE: 4″ diameter × 1¼″ tall

Many cultures view ladybugs as lucky, and a great deal of superstition surrounds these small and stylishly outfitted insects.

Be sure to count the number of spots on your lucky ladybug. The spots represent the number of years of good luck that await you!

If the ladybug takes off toward your little finger, you're about to get good news.

If it lands on your ring finger, you'll receive a marriage proposal!

If the ladybug lands on your left hand (your "heart" hand), you'll have many years of love.

In Argentina, ladybugs are called *Vaquitas de San Antonio*. The legend is that St. Anthony tried to stop a cow that was about to stomp on a ladybug nest. For his trouble, St. Anthony received a nasty kick from the cow!

For this project, I used Sunspots in red by Amy Butler for Rowan Fabrics and Palette in black by Marcia Derse for Windham Fabrics.

CONSTRUCTION OVERVIEW: Tulle wings create the illusion of delicate wings on this whimsical ladybug. Layered buttons give this bug a wide-eyed, cartoony look. Simple points on the black head section form "antennae."

Materials Requirements and Cutting Instructions

Ladybug Pincushion

FABRIC	FOR	CUTTING
7″ × 7″ scrap, fat quarter, or ¼ yard of polka dot	Body	Cut 1 piece using template C.
7″ × 7″ scrap, fat quarter, or ¼ yard of black solid	Head	Cut 1 piece 7″ × 7″.
7″ × 14″ white tulle	Wings	Cut 2 pieces using template B.
Felt scrap at least 4″ × 4″ square	Base	Use pinking shears to cut 1 piece using template E.

FINDINGS: ½ oz. polyester fiberfill, 4″ round chipboard coaster (or stiff cardboard trimmed into a 4″ circle using template D), extra-strong thread in any color, 2 white buttons ⅓″ wide, 2 black sequins ¼″ wide, 2 black beads, 2 straight pins

TOOLS: Sewing machine, clear template plastic, fabric marker, pinking shears, regular scissors, turning tool, hot-glue gun and sticks, white glue

Find Ladybug Pincushion marking template A and Patterns B, C, D, and E on pullout page P1. Trace onto clear template plastic and cut out to create templates A, B, C, D, and E.

For more information about the supplies needed for this project, see My Sewing Necessities (page 14). For information about where to buy materials, see Resources (page 143).

The Ladybug Pincushion will make you smile as she sits near your sewing machine and holds your pins. What about gifting a Ladybug Pincushion with a copy of the "legend" attached?

Getting It Together

BODY ASSEMBLY

1. To make the head piece, fold black fabric in half, right sides together. Trace marking template A onto the fabric with a fabric marker. With black thread, sew directly on top of the line indicated by the dotted line on the pattern. With pinking shears, trim the seam allowance to ¼″ and trim the corners straight across. Use regular scissors to cut directly on the remaining traced lines. Turn right side out and push the corners out with a turning tool.

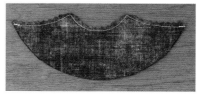

With black thread (white thread used here for contrast only), sew a line directly on top of the marked line.

2. Place the polka dot body circle right side up on a work surface. Lay the folded tulle fabric pieces on top of the circle. Match the raw edges of tulle to the raw edges of the body fabric, with the top corners of tulle touching. Place the black fabric headpiece on top of the body fabric and tulle, centering it on top of the section where the tulle meets. Pin.

Tip

Tulle can be tricky to work with. Use at least two pins to affix the template to the tulle when preparing the wings. Put a piece of light-colored scrap paper under the tulle when you trace on it to protect your work surface.

3. Thread a needle with 24″ extra-strong thread and knot the end. Backstitch (page 12) at the bottom of the assembled pieces, then stitch ¼″ from the edge, using a ¼″ stitch length completely around the perimeter. Do not backstitch or cut the thread.

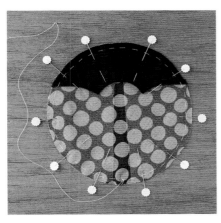

Stitch completely around perimeter with a ¼″ stitch, ¼″ from edge.

4. Place the assembled ladybug facedown on a work surface. Place a handful of polyester fiberfill onto the center of the circle. Place a coaster (or cardboard base cut from template D) onto the fiberfill. Press down to compress the fiberfill and draw the thread to pull the fabric around the coaster about ½″. Backstitch, knot, and trim the thread.

Pull the fabric around the coaster about ½″.

5. Hot-glue felt to the ladybug bottom to cover the coaster or cardboard and the fabric's raw edges.

Hot-glue felt onto the bottom of the assembly.

FACE DETAILS

1. For the antennae, thread each of 2 straight pins with a black seed bead. Apply a bit of white glue to the pin shaft. Insert into the points of black fabric.

2. For the eyes, thread each of 2 straight pins with a black sequin, then a button. Audition placement of the eyes on the ladybug face. Pull the pins out slightly, then add a bit of white glue to the shaft under the buttons. Push the pins back in place. Let dry.

Finish the antennae and eyes with straight pins, buttons, sequins, beads, and a bit of white glue.

Kissing Flowers Needle Case

FINISHED SIZE: 4½″ × 2½″

Imagine whipping out the sweetest lil needle case at your next sewing get-together. And on top of it, there are tiny pincushions to safeguard your pins and needle—stylin'! And what great gifts...

For this project, I used Flutter and Flowers by Laura Berringer for Marcus Fabrics, Gelato by Daiwabo for E.E. Schenck, and a Liberty of London print from my stash.

CONSTRUCTION OVERVIEW: Sew two layers of fabric onto an elongated yin-yang shape. Add fusible shapes for stiffness. Turn right side out. Finish fusing and topstitch. Add a wool felt rectangle to house the needles. Make 3D stuffed flowers and glue them to interlocking flaps for decoration—and to serve as mini pincushions!

Materials Requirements and Cutting Instructions

Kissing Flowers Needle Case

FABRIC	FOR	CUTTING
⅛ yard each of 2 coordinating fabrics	Outer needle case	Cut 2 rectangles 3″ × 7″ from each fabric.
4″ × 8″ rectangle of coordinating fabric	Flowers	Cut 2 circles using template E.
3″ × 14″ rectangle of heavy-duty, double-sided fusible interfacing or 3 scraps 2½″ × 4½″ (I used Craf-Tex Plus. You could also use fast2fuse HEAVY.)	Interfacing	Cut 1 piece each using templates B, C, and D.
3″ × 5″ scrap of wool felt in coordinating color	Needle holder	

FINDINGS: 6 small iridescent beads for flower centers, regular thread to coordinate with beads, approximately ½ oz. premium polyester fiberfill

TOOLS: Sewing machine, iron, clear template plastic, nonstick ironing sheet, gluestick, seam ripper, turning tool, Fray Check

Find Kissing Flower Needle Case marking template A and Patterns B, C, D, and E on pullout page P1. Trace onto clear template plastic and cut out to create templates A, B, C, D, and E.

For more information about the products used in this project, see My Sewing Necessities (page 14). For ordering information, see Resources (page 143).

The Kissing Flowers Needle Case will keep your pins and needles in style and is small enough to tuck into your sewing kit. Use the flowers for tiny pincushions when you are sewing on the go!

Getting It Together

CASE BODY

1. Pin a 3″ × 7″ rectangle for the outer needle case right sides together with a 3″ × 7″ rectangle from the second coordinating fabric. Sew a short side of each pair with a ¼″ seam. Press the seam open. Repeat with the other pair of rectangles.

2. Place the units from Step 1 right sides together, matching like fabrics, and pin at the seams. Center template A and trace onto the fabric sandwich.

3. With a short machine stitch, sew completely around the drawn shape. Cut out, leaving a ¼″ seam allowance. Clip curves and corners. Apply Fray Check to the inner corners.

Each flap will be a different color.

4. On 1 side of the unit, arrange fusible shapes B, C, and D within ⅛″ of borders. Secure in place with a bit of glue.

5. Turn the unit facedown on a nonstick ironing sheet. Press with a hot, steamy iron to affix the fusible interfacing to the fabric. Let cool. Peel away from the nonstick sheet.

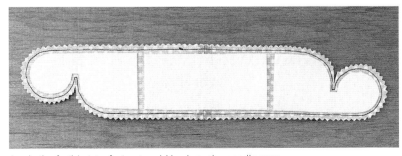

Apply the fusible interfacing to add body to the needle case.

6. On 1 side of the unit (this will become the inside, covered by felt), use a seam ripper to carefully unsew (page 12) a 1½″ turning slit in the seam. Carefully turn the unit right side out through slit. Push out the curves with a turning tool.

Open a turning slit in the seam with a seam ripper.

7. Bring the edges of the turning slit together. Press to fuse all the fabric to the fusible.

8. Center the felt square over the slit in the needle case. Hot-glue in place.

Use pure wool felt; needles love it.

FLOWER ACCENTS

1. Use a single strand of coordinating heavy thread to sew all the way around both circle E pieces. Start by taking a backstitch, then stitch ⅛″ from the raw edge using a ¼″ stitch length. Start and end on the right side of the fabric. Do not backstitch at the end.

Sew around the circle. Dark thread used here for contrast only.

2. Gather the circle up into a cup shape. Insert a piece of fiberfill, and pull the thread tight to close the circle. Tie off but don't cut the thread. Press to flatten the puff.

Stuffed puff, ready to cinch up

3. Starting from the back side of the puff, bring the needle up through the center of the puff. Wrap the thread around to the back side of the puff and bring the needle up through the same hole. Wrap again in the same position and pull the thread tight. Move to the next position and repeat the wrap stitches until you have 6 "clefts" around the perimeter of the puff. Do not tie off or cut the thread before the next step.

Pull tight for voluptuous puffs.

4. Using the same thread, bring it up through the center of the puff. Thread a bead on, and stitch back down through the center. Repeat for the 2 remaining beads. Tie off in back and clip the threads.

Sew beads on one at a time.

5. Fold the flaps of the needle case over the felt and hook them together. Hot-glue flowers onto the rounded sections of the flaps so that the flowers almost touch.

Audition the flower puff placement before gluing in place.

Cloisonné Catch-All Bowl

FINISHED SIZE: 9˝ diameter × 4˝ tall

No one has ever accused me of being neat, but I do swear by keeping a container on my sewing table to hold stray threads and fabric bits. Not only will this bowl hold your scraps as you sew, but its puffy sides will also corral your needles and pins!

Fabric choice makes these look especially fabulous. I used Shagreen from A Closer Look by La Todera for Clothworks and Zigzag by Keiko Goke for Yuwa Fabrics.

P.S. These make fantastic gifts, even for the nonsewing bunch! Cloisonné Catch-All Bowls are great for holding jewelry, office supplies, hair accessories, and more!

CONSTRUCTION OVERVIEW: Padded circles are joined at alternating points and stuffed with fabric beads. The distention of the borders forms the circles into a bowl.

Materials Requirements and Cutting Instructions

Cloisonné Catch-All Bowl

FABRIC	FOR	CUTTING
¾ yard dark patterned fabric	Framework	Cut 6 squares 10½″ × 10½″.
⅓ yard or 16 charm squares	Puffs	Cut 16 squares 5″ × 5″.
⅓ yard Pellon Fusible Fleece #987, 45″ wide	Padding	Cut 3 squares 10½″ × 10½″.

FINDINGS: Machine sewing thread and extra-strong hand-sewing thread to match the framework fabric, 5 oz. polyester fiberfill

TOOLS: Sewing machine with walking foot, clear template plastic, pinking shears, disappearing-ink fabric marker, turning tool, hot-glue gun and sticks

Find Cloisonné Catch-All Bowl marking templates A and B on pullout page P2. Trace onto template plastic, transfer all markings, and cut out to create templates A and B.

For more information about the supplies needed for this project, see My Sewing Necessities (page 14). For information about where to buy materials, see Resources (page 143).

The Cloisonné Catch-All Bowl can hold sewing notions, jewelry, coins, or jelly beans!

Getting It Together

FRAMEWORK

1. Center template A on the wrong side of 3 squares of framework fabric and trace with disappearing ink.

2. Make 3 stacks in the following order:

- Bottom: 10½″ square fusible fleece, placed fusible (rough) side down

- Middle: 10½″ square of fabric, right side up

- Top: 10½″ square of fabric, right side down (marked with template A circle)

3. Pin through all layers in the center of each stack.

4. Using a walking foot, sew completely around the outline.

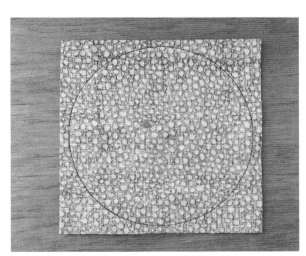

Sew directly on top of the template A outline. Your machine's walking foot will keep the layers from shifting.

5. Using pinking shears, trim excess fabric ¼″ from the stitching.

6. Pinch the stack to separate the top layer of fabric. Carefully cut a 1″ slit (top layer of fabric only) in the center of the top circle. Repeat for the remaining 2 units.

To create a turning slit, clip through the top layer of fabric only.

7. Turn the unit right side out through the slit. Insert a turning tool into the slit and smooth the curves.

8. Pinch the edges of the slit together. Press with a hot iron to fuse. Continue pressing the circle to fuse the fabric completely to the fusible fleece.

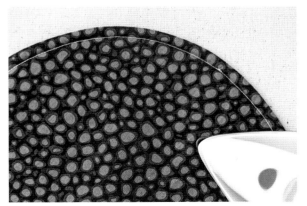

Iron the fabric to the fusible fleece to close the turning slit.

9. Using matching thread, topstitch ¼″ from the edge of all 3 pancakes.

10. Pin the 3 units together, facing the slit sides toward the inside layers. Using template B, trace a circle with a disappearing-ink marker in the center of the top unit.

11. Stitch on top of the traced circle through all layers.

12. Using the black dots on template A as a guide, mark the top layer of the stacked circles by inserting a straight pin directly into the top-stitching at each black dot. These points are where you will tack the top and middle rows of the unit together.

13. Turn the unit over and carefully line up the black dots on template A with the pins you have inserted on the top of the unit. Using the gray dots as a guide, mark points on the bottom of the unit with straight pins that are different from the pins you used on the top. These points are where you will tack the middle and bottom rows of the unit together.

When you are finished, the top points should be halfway between the points on the bottom.

Yellow pins mark the joins of the top and middle layers. Orange pins mark the joins of the middle and bottom layers.

14. Use the bar tack stitch on your machine to join the top and middle layers together at the 8 marked intersections. Sew directly on top of the top stitching, folding the bottom layer out of the way as needed.

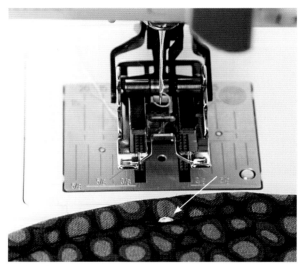
Tack the layers in an alternating pattern to create a honeycomb effect.

Tip

Not sure what a bar tack stitch is? Just use a zigzag stitch on a narrow setting with the shortest stitch length.

15. Flip the unit over and repeat the tacking process to tack the middle and bottom layers, following the marks you have made on the bottom of the unit.

PUFFS

1. For each puff, cut a 12″ length of extra-strong thread. Knot the end. Starting on the right side of a 5″ square, take a backstitch. Continue stitching ⅛″ from the raw edge of the fabric around the perimeter of the square, using a ¼″ stitch length.

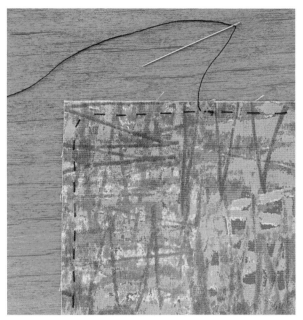

Keep your stitches even as you stitch around the square.

2. Draw up the thread slightly to cup the fabric. Stuff tightly with fiberfill until the puff is as firm as a grape. Draw up the thread completely. Backstitch, knot, and trim the thread. Repeat this step for all 16 puffs.

Stuff puffs, then stuff some more, until they have the firmness of a grape.

BOWL ASSEMBLY

1. Squash the puffs slightly to fit the diamond-shaped cavities. Position each puff into an open space on the side of the bowl's framework. Audition the placement until you are happy with the composition. Pin in place.

2. Remove puffs 1 at a time and apply hot glue ½″ inside the border of each cavity. Replace the puffs and hold in place until the glue cools.

Apply glue and replace puffs one at a time to preserve the shape of the bowl.

Done!

Just for Yo—

Just for you—and your favorite people, that is! These projects are super wearable *and* giftable! Customize to go with every ensemble—these trinkets will flatter everyone. Treat yourself or a friend!

Gum-Wrapper Weave Fabric Cuff

FINISHED SIZE: 8″ circumference; cuff, 2¾″ wide;
single bracelet, 1⅛″ wide

The durable, glam version of gum-wrapper chains! Perfect to show off
your favorite precut strip bundle fabrics.

For this project, I used Shot Cottons by Kaffe Fassett for Rowan Fabrics
and Anna Maria Horner fabrics for Free Spirit Fabrics.

CONSTRUCTION OVERVIEW: Apply heavy-duty fusible to
fabric strips. Fold and set creases with a hot iron. Weave
links into a bracelet. String two single-chain bracelets
together to make a cuff!

Materials Requirements and Cutting Instructions

Gum-Wrapper Weave Fabric Cuff

FABRIC	FOR	CUTTING
2½″ pre-cut strips of assorted fabrics, ¼ yard or fat quarter for each chain	Single-chain cuff (2 chains)	Cut 18 strips 2½″ × 6″.
		Cut 36 strips 2½″ × 6″.
⅝ yard for single chain, 1⅜ yards for cuff of heavyweight paper-backed fusible webbing such as HeatnBond Ultrahold, 17″ wide	Single-chain cuff (2 chains)	Cut 18 strips 2½″ × 6″.
		Cut 36 strips 2½″ × 6″.

FINDINGS: Extra-strong thread, small paper clip

TOOLS: Iron, nonstick ironing surface such as Silicone Release Paper (by C&T Publishing)

For more information about the supplies needed for this project, see My Sewing Necessities (page 14). For information about where to buy materials, see Resources (page 143).

The Gum-Wrapper Weave Fabric Cuff can also be made as a single chain.

Getting It Together

LINKS

Prepare all strips at the same time, assembly-line style.

1. With a hot, dry iron, fuse the heavyweight webbing to the wrong side of the fabric strips. *Leave the paper on the strips.*

Tip

To avoid gumming up your iron with fusible webbing, work on a nonstick ironing surface. Lightly tack the fusible webbing to fabric to hold it in place. Cover your strips with another nonstick sheet or a piece of aluminum foil. Fuse.

2. Fold all strips in half lengthwise, with fabric on the outside. Finger-press, then press with an iron.

Fold in half lengthwise. Don't remove the paper backing from the fusible.

3. Fold both long edges in to meet at the center crease. Finger-press, then press with an iron.

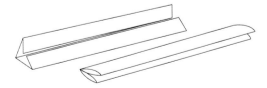

4. Fold in half widthwise. Finger-press, then press with an iron.

5. Open, then fold the short ends in to the center fold. Finger-press, then press with an iron.

6. Press the unit again with an iron to lock it in shape.

7. Repeat Steps 1–6 to make 18 links for a single bracelet or 36 for a cuff.

8. Let the shapes cool thoroughly and then, finally, carefully remove the paper. (You know you've been dying to!)

CHAIN ASSEMBLY

1. Choose the first link.

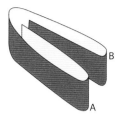

2. Insert points C and D of a second link into slots A and B of the first link and pull it through.

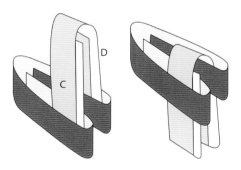

3. Add a third link, inserting the tabs into the slots visible in the second link.

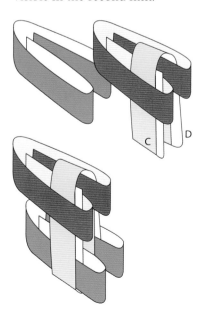

4. Continue to add links in the same manner until you have added all 18 links to the chain.

5. To connect the 2 ends of the chain, start by unfolding the last 2 folds of the last link you added to the chain.

6. Wrap the ends of the link you have just undone over both outside edges of the first link on the opposite end of the chain. Insert the raw edges of the undone link into the slots in the first link. (You'll be doing the same thing you've been doing all along, but backward.) Pull the ends through until you reach the original folded point.

> ## Tip
> Use a paper clip or a similar item to push the links through on this step.

7. If you want to make a cuff, make 2 chains.

CUFF ASSEMBLY

Although you will use thread to connect the rows of links together, it's not really sewing (piercing the fabric). It's simply weaving thread through the folds in the links.

1. Tie a 24″ length of extra-strong thread onto 1 end of a small paper clip.

2. Place 2 single-row chains together, 1 on top of the other, fitting the peaks of the bottom bracelet into the valleys of the top chain.

3. Slide the paper clip through a joint in the top bracelet as shown in the cuff assembly diagram (below). Leave a 6″ tail of thread sticking out.

4. Thread a paper clip through the adjacent link on the bottom bracelet.

5. Continue joining the links of both bracelets in this fashion until you reach the link you first passed the thread through. Give the thread a tug to make sure the thread is sitting snugly in the folds and the bracelets are joined firmly together. Tie the loose ends of the thread in a tight surgeon's knot (page 13). Weave in the ends of the thread and trim the extra thread.

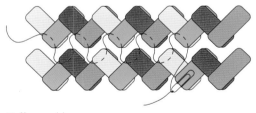

Cuff assembly

Done!

Zaftig Zinnia Brooch

FINISHED SIZE: 6″ diameter × 2″ thick

Who doesn't love zinnias? In nature, they come in just about every color under the sun, so make them in any color you like using one of the many ombré fabrics now on the market. I used different colorways from the Gelato collection by Daiwabo for E.E. Schenck to make a variety of zinnia brooches.

This oversized bloom is a gorgeous statement piece for your jean jacket, handbag, and even bridesmaid dress. Simple to make, stunning to wear!

CONSTRUCTION OVERVIEW: Cut lemon-shaped petals in color order from ombré fabric. Fold, stitch, and string each petal onto a single thread. Use hot glue to attach the petal chain to a spiral drawn on a puffed fabric base. Add a felt backing and a bar pin.

Materials Requirements and Cutting Instructions

Zaftig Zinnia

FABRIC	FOR	CUTTING
½ yard ombré fabric with colors running selvage to selvage	Petals	Fold fabric in half, selvage to selvage, matching the ombré pattern. Cut 4 strips 2¾″ × width of fabric.
	Base	Cut 1 piece from the midtone of the ombré using template B1.
5″ × 7″ rectangle of felt	Backing	Cut 1 piece each using templates C and E with pinking shears.

FINDINGS: Extra-strong thread to match the lightest petal color, scraps of polyester fiberfill, 4″ round chipboard coaster or stiff cardboard cut with pattern C, a 1¼″ bar pin back

TOOLS: Clear template plastic, masking tape or small plain stickers, pencil, carbon or transfer paper for fabric, plain white paper, pinking shears, hot-glue gun and sticks

Find Zaftig Zinnia patterns A, B1, C, D, and E, and marking template B2, on pullout page P2. Trace onto clear template plastic and cut out to create templates A, B1, C, D, and E. Photocopy or trace marking template B2 onto plain white paper.

For more information about the supplies needed for this project, see My Sewing Necessities (page 14). For information about where to buy materials, see Resources (page 143).

By using an ombré print, a single cut of fabric is all you need to get all of the graduated petal colors in the Zaftig Zinnia Brooch.

Getting It Together

PETALS

1. Neatly stack folded fabric strips, matching selvages. Trace template A at an angle onto the fabric 8 times, with the shapes barely touching. Pin through the center of each drawn shape. Use a sticker or small piece of tape to number circles 1–8 from dark to light.

Number petal shapes to keep the shading in order.

2. Cut out the petals. You will have 8 petals in each stack. Keep stacks pinned. Set aside 2 petals from stack 8 for the flower center (page 96).

Shaded petals in order

Tip

If you are not using a broadly shaded ombré fabric, you do not need to number or keep petal stacks in order.

3. Thread a needle with a 48″ length of heavy thread and knot the end. Unpin stack 1. Finger-press a petal in half lengthwise. Starting at 1 corner of the raw edges, take ¼″ stitches ⅛″ from the fabric edge. Start and end the stitching on the top of the petal. Do not backstitch. Push the petal down the thread toward the knot.

Stitch evenly along raw edges, starting and stopping on top of petal.

4. Fold and add the remaining petals in stack 1 to the thread, then fold and add the petals from the remaining stacks in numerical order.

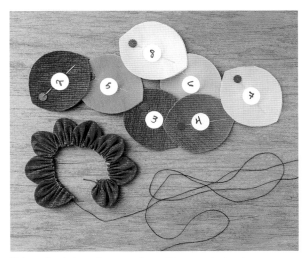

String all petals on the same thread in numerical order.

5. From the knot, measure exactly 42″ and mark the end of the thread. Gather the petals along the thread until all the petals fit between the knot and the 42″ mark. Backstitch to secure the last petal to this point. Trim the threads. Distribute the fullness of the petals, adjusting the gathers.

Take your time finessing the petals and distributing the tiny gathers.

FLOWER CENTER

1. Trim a reserved petal from stack 8 into a circle using template D. Fold the raw edge over ¼″ to the wrong side. With matching thread, backstitch once, then stitch around the perimeter ⅛″ from the edge with an ⅛″ stitch length, as if you were making a traditional yo-yo.

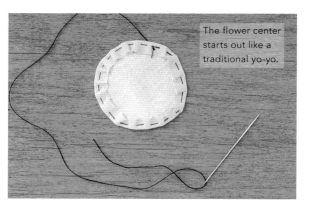

The flower center starts out like a traditional yo-yo.

2. Draw the thread up slightly and stuff the center with fiberfill. Pull the thread tighter to close the gap. Backstitch, knot, and trim the thread.

3. Repeat Step 1 with the remaining petal from stack 8. Place the stitched circle facedown. Place the puff completed in Step 2, gathered side down, on the stitched circle. Draw the thread from the stitched circle up around the puff, stopping when there is a ½″ gap in the center. Carefully backstitch, knot, and bury the thread. Set aside.

Finished stuffed yo-yo, gathered side down, wrapped with unstuffed yo-yo, gathered side up

BASE

1. Center paper template B2 onto the right side of circle B1. Pin in place and trace around the perimeter. Place carbon paper under the template and trace the spiral onto the fabric.

Trace B2 spiral onto B1 pattern piece.

2. Thread a needle with a 24″ length of heavy thread and knot. Backstitch, then stitch around the perimeter of the circle with a ¼″ stitch about ¼″ from the edge. When finished, do not backstitch or cut the thread.

3. Place the circle facedown. Place a handful of fiberfill onto the center of the circle. Place the coaster (or cardboard base cut from template C) onto the fiberfill. Press down and draw the thread up to pull the fabric around the coaster. Backstitch, knot, and trim the thread.

Gathered and stuffed spiral base

FLOWER ASSEMBLY

1. Arrange the outermost round of petals on the spiral, starting at the edge of the dome and stopping short of the second round of the spiral. Do not cut the thread. Pin at least every other petal. Apply a bead of hot glue to join the raw edge of the petals to the base. Let cool and then remove the pins.

Apply the first round of petals to the dome base, following a spiral pattern.

2. Arrange the second round of petals on the dome. Glue. Repeat until you reach the center of the spiral. Use hot glue to attach the flower center, covering the last raw edges of the petals.

Attach the puffed flower center, covering the raw edges of the center petals.

3. Use hot glue to attach the large felt circle onto the back of the flower base.

4. Open the bar pin and spread a scant amount of hot glue onto the section with the holes. Immediately press the smaller circle of felt onto the pin, centering the pin.

5. Apply more glue to the back side of the small circle covering the pin. Center 1″ from the border onto the large felt circle on the back of the flower.

Glue a small pinked felt circle over the bar pin for a neat appearance.

6. Check for any gaps between petal rows and touch up with hot glue.

Done!

Water Lily Brooches

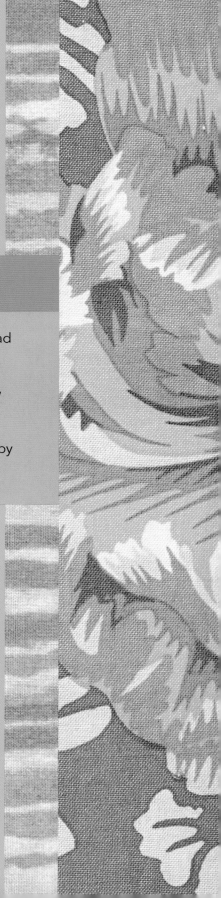

FINISHED SIZES: Large: 5½˝ diameter × 2˝ thick; Medium: 4½˝ × 2˝ thick; Small: 3½˝ × 2˝ thick

These Water Lily Brooches are the perfect complement to the Lily Pad Centerpiece (page 44).

Of course they'd make perfectly lovely wearable brooches, too. How about for a summer wedding?

For this project, I used white Kona PFD (prepared-for-dyeing) fabric by Robert Kaufman.

CONSTRUCTION OVERVIEW: Cut 25 circles from fabric. Fold and press each petal, then string onto extra-strong thread lengths to form two petal rings. Create a fabric cone for the center bud, then glue all elements together and add a pin.

Materials Requirements and Cutting Instructions

Water Lily Brooches

FABRIC	FOR	CUTTING
¾ yard white PFD fabric	Large brooch	Cut 4 strips 5″ × width of fabric.
		Cut 25 circles using template A.
½ yard	Medium brooch	Cut 3 strips 4″ × width of fabric.
		Cut 25 circles using template B.
¼ yard	Small brooch	Cut 2 strips 3″ × width of fabric.
		Cut 25 circles using template C.
4″ × 10″ rectangle of felt (to make all 3 brooches)	Brooch backing and bar pin backing	Use pinking shears to cut the following:
	Large brooch	Cut 1 piece using template D.
4″ × 4″ square of felt (for 1 brooch)	Medium brooch	Cut 1 piece using template E.
	Small brooch	Cut 1 piece using template F.
	All brooches	Cut 1 piece using template G.

FINDINGS: Strong thread such as Gütermann's Extra-Strong Thread in white, 1¼″ bar pin for each brooch

TOOLS: Clear template plastic, hot-glue gun and sticks, nonstick gluing sheet, pinking shears, Ranger alcohol inks in Wild Plum and Stream, rubbing alcohol, spray bottle, paintbrush

Find Water Lily Brooches Patterns A, B, C, D, E, F, and G on pullout page P1. Trace onto clear template plastic and cut out to create templates A, B, C, D, E, F, and G.

For more information about the supplies needed for this project, see My Sewing Necessities (page 14). For information about where to buy materials, see Resources (page 143).

Make Water Lily Brooches in any of three sizes to wear or to embellish the Lily Pad Centerpiece (page 44).

Getting It Together

PETAL RINGS

Note: Follow instructions for all sizes.

1. Press all circles in half. Fold both corners in to meet at the center of the curve. Press.

Fold the circle in half and bring the corners to the center.

2. Thread a needle with a 24″ length of strong thread. Knot the thread, leaving a 6″ tail. With a ¼″ stitch, stitch ⅛″ from the raw edge of the curve, starting and stopping on the folded side of the circle. Do not backstitch or knot.

Tip

Contrary to one's "sewing intuition," it's important not to make your stitches too small when threading the petals, or they will not scrunch up enough for Step 4. For small petals, take three in-and-out stitches. For medium petals (above right), take four stitches. For large petals, take six stitches.

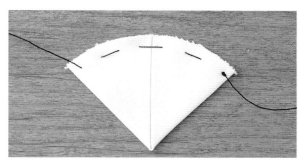

Add the first petal to the gathering thread. Use matching thread; dark thread used here for contrast only. (Medium petal shown.)

3. Continue to add petals to the gathering thread until you have added 16 petals.

4. From the knot, measure 8″ for a large petal ring, 6″ for a medium, and 4¾″ for a small and mark the thread. Gather the petals along the thread until all the petals fit between the knot and the mark on the thread. Backstitch, then knot to secure the last petal in this ring. Trim the threads. Distribute the fullness of the petals, adjusting gathers.

Large petal ring

5. Use the same method to make the small petal ring, except thread a needle with an 18″ length of strong thread and knot it, leaving a 6″ tail. Add 8 petals to the thread. To gather the small petal ring, measure from the knot 4½″ for a large brooch, 3¾″ for a medium, and 2¼″ for a small.

Small petal ring

BUD CONE

1. Fold the remaining circle in half. Finger-press. Fold the circle again (into quarters), matching creases and raw edges. Finger-press. Open the last fold. You will have a half-circle with a bisecting crease.

2. Using white thread and a short stitch length (2.0), sew along the creased line, backstitching at the beginning and end. Cut the threads and trim.

Stitch directly on the crease lines of the semicircle. Black thread used for contrast only.

3. Invert half of the circle over the other half to form a 2-layer fabric cone, right side out.

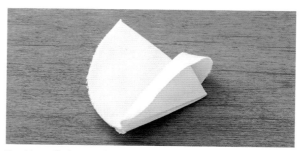

Double-walled center bud cone

4. Thread a needle with at least a 12″ length of strong thread. Backstitch (page 12), then stitch around the perimeter ⅛″ from the raw edge through both layers of the fabric cone using a ¼″ stitch length.

5. Draw the thread up slightly and stuff firmly with polyester fiberfill. Stuff the cone very firmly; think the firmness of a grape!

6. Draw up the thread to close the opening completely. Backstitch, knot, and trim the thread.

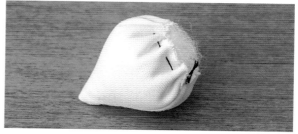

Stuffed center bud cone

BROOCH ASSEMBLY

1. Shape each petal by pressing the center gently with your thumb. Pull every other petal up and forward, toward the center of the ring, to add dimension to the petal layer.

Finesse the petals to make the look more realistic.

2. *For fabric dyeing, be sure to wear safety glasses and a mask and work in a well-ventilated area.* To tint petals, mist petal rings thoroughly with rubbing alcohol. Dilute a few drops of Ranger alcohol inks with rubbing alcohol—3 drops Wild Plum and 1 drop Stream per teaspoon of alcohol. Apply sparingly to the tips of the petals and the center bud with a paintbrush. Add a bit more color to the center portions of the flower for a more realistic effect. Let dry.

3. Arrange the large petal circle on a nonstick gluing surface. Apply hot glue to the inner edges of the ring.

4. Center the small petal ring on top of the large petal ring. Press into place until the glue is cool.

5. Glue the fabric cone to the center.

6. Use hot glue to attach the felt circle onto the back of the brooch.

7. Open the bar pin and spread a scant amount of hot glue onto the section with the holes. Immediately press the smaller circle of felt onto the pin, centering the pin.

8. Apply more glue to the back side of the small circle covering the pin. Center 1″ from the border onto the large felt circle on the back of the flower.

Glue a small circle of felt over the bar pin for a neat finish.

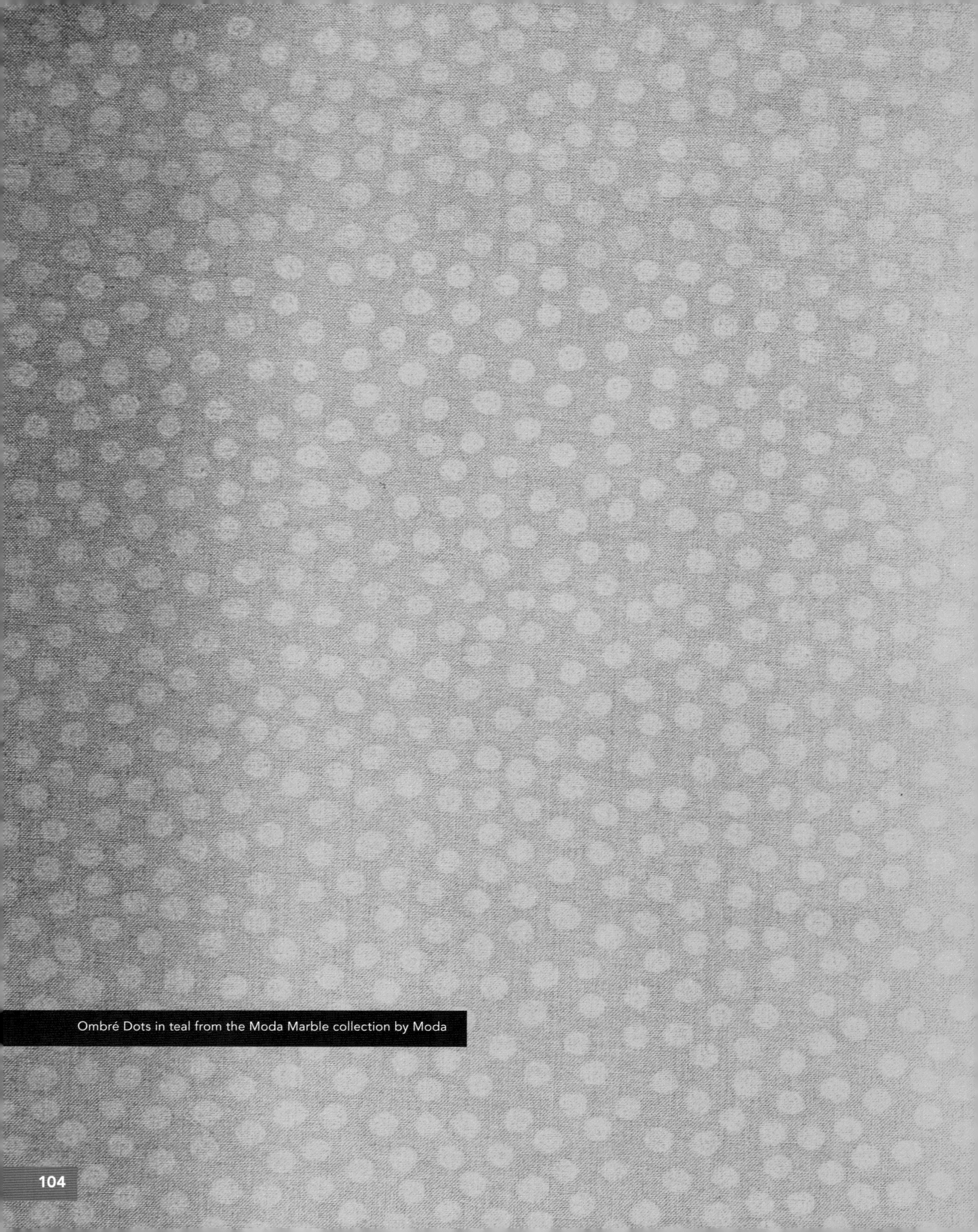

Ombré Dots in teal from the Moda Marble collection by Moda

For the Holidays

Looking for something a little different to craft for the holidays? Look no more! Three projects to give a unique, cosmopolitan look to your holiday decor and gift "wrapping." These projects are reusable, future heirlooms! Get into the holiday spirit!

Lavish
Lantern
Ornament

FINISHED SIZE: 3⅝″ diameter × 10″ long, including hanger

From the souks of Tangier to your Christmas tree. If you are looking to "open a can of exotic" on your holiday decor, this is your project. Make several and keep these lanterns out all year as key tassels, scissor fobs, and chandelier decorations!

For this project, I used Kaffe Fassett Collective fabrics for Westminster and Marcia Derse Palette tonals for Windham Fabrics.

CONSTRUCTION OVERVIEW: Sew tubes of fabric in three sizes. Gather each end, stuff, and close. Tuft with coordinating colors of embroidery thread. String together, then add a tassel and a hanging loop.

Materials Requirements and Cutting Instructions

Lavish Lantern Ornament

FABRIC	FOR	CUTTING
1 fat quarter or ¼ yard floral print	Lantern center	Cut 1 strip 6″ × 12″.
1 fat quarter or ¼ yard small or tonal print	Middle discs	Cut 2 strips 3″ × 6″.
	Top and bottom caps of lantern	Cut 2 strips 1½″ × 3″.

FINDINGS: Extra-strong thread in any color, large handful of premium polyester fiberfill, 2 skeins of embroidery floss in coordinating colors (1 for sectioning puffs, 1 for tassel and hanger)

TOOLS: Sewing machine; rotary cutter, ruler, and mat; long needle such as a doll needle, white craft glue

For more information about the supplies needed for this project, see My Sewing Necessities (page 14). For information about where to buy materials, see Resources (page 143).

Make the Lavish Lantern Ornament in a variety of colors to add an exotic feel to your holiday tree. Use the ornaments year-round as tassels to decorate a favorite piece of furniture, a doorknob, or even a keychain!

Getting It Together

LANTERN PUFFS

1. Fold all strips cut from both fabrics in half widthwise, right sides together. Using a small machine stitch (2.0), sew raw edges together with a ¼″ seam.

2. Finger-press the seam open and fold 1 edge down ¼″. Finger-press. Thread a needle with strong thread and knot the end. Sew a ⅛″ gathering stitch close to the edge.

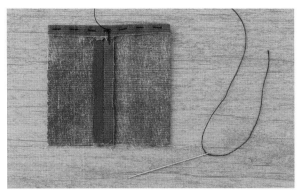

Sew a gathering stitch around the edge.

3. Draw up the thread to close the opening. Knot and trim the thread.

Pull thread to close the opening.

4. Fold the remaining raw edge over ¼″. Knot the thread end again and sew a small running stitch close to the edge.

Add a gathering stitch; almost ready to stuff.

5. Turn the tube right side out, and insert a needle through the seam to bring the thread to the right side of the fabric.

Ready to stuff

6. Stuff the tube tightly with polyester fiberfill. Draw up the thread to close the opening. Backstitch, knot, and trim the thread.

Basic lantern part

7. Thread a sharp embroidery needle with a 36″ full strand of embroidery floss. Tie a large knot at the end. Starting from the center of the side opposite the gathering stitches, bring a needle up through the center, catching a few threads on the border of the gathered edge to secure. Wrap the thread around to the back of the puff, over the seamline from Step 1, and bring the needle up through the same hole. Pull tight. Repeat in the same place.

Tip

Wrap the embroidery floss around each section twice. This will help tighten the thread and make deeper indents.

Cuuute! It's a baby pumpkin shape!

10. Repeat Steps 2–9 with the remaining seamed strips.

Be sure to wrap floss tightly to "lift and separate" sections for a more voluptuous puff!

Finished puffs for one lantern

8. Wrap the floss around to the opposite side of the puff, again wrapping twice.

9. Continue wrapping the floss around the puff, dividing each half into 2 sections, then in half again. When you are finished, you should have 8 wedge-shaped sections. Knot the floss, bury the ends, and trim. Your puff should now resemble a baby pumpkin that looks identical on both sides.

TASSEL AND HANGER

1. Remove the paper from an embroidery floss hank. Wrap the floss around 4 fingers 12 times. Slide off your fingers. Cut.

Fingers are your "handiest" tool!

2. Cut 2 full 8″ strands from the remaining floss. Tie the top of the floss you wound around your fingers with 1 of the strands.

Smooth the floss together. Use the remaining 8″ length of floss to tie off ⅝″ from the top.

Tip

To make the ties lie flat with the rest of the tassel, thread a needle with the ends of the floss ties and bring them down through the center of the tassel.

3. Trim the ends of the tassel straight across, about 3″ from the top of the tassel.

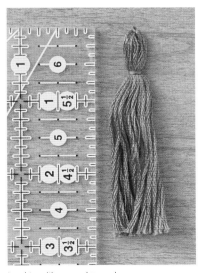

Looking like a real tassel now

4. To make a hanging loop, cut 3 full 12″ strands of embroidery floss. Braid these 3 strands of floss and knot all loose ends together.

ASSEMBLY

1. Thread a long doll needle with a 24″ length of strong thread. Thread the sections of the ornament onto the thread in the following order: small puff, medium puff, large puff, medium puff, small puff, and through the head of the tassel.

Bring the thread back up through all sections to the top of the ornament.

Thread through the hanging loop and tie the ends of the thread tightly in a surgeon's knot (page 13). Bring the ends of the thread through the side of the puff to bury them. Trim.

Thread the lantern parts together.

2. To keep parts of the ornament from shifting, part the layers gently and apply a few drops of white glue between the layers.

Done! Now go make a zillion!

Puffy Tabletop Christmas Trees

FINISHED SIZES: Large: 6″ diameter × 7″ tall;
Medium: 5″ diameter × 5½″ tall;
Small: 4″ diameter × 4½″ tall

Made of puffy fabric cones, these fun-to-make, kid-friendly Christmas decorations would be great for a tabletop display. Make one or three; one in each size. These could be seriously blinged out with pompons, beads, or sequins. Or leave them plain for a modern look!

CONSTRUCTION OVERVIEW: Make nineteen fabric cones crafted from circles. Gather, stuff, and string them together into consecutively sized rings. Glue rings together and add a felt base.

Materials Requirements and Cutting Instructions

For this project, I used Moda Ombré Dots fabric in teal. I cut each tree from a different section of the yardage so that each would look slightly different.

Puffy Tabletop Christmas Trees

FABRIC	FOR	CUTTING
⅞ yard fabric	Large tree	Cut 19 circles using template A.
⅝ yard fabric	Medium tree	Cut 19 circles using template B.
⅜ yard fabric	Small tree	Cut 19 circles using template C.
Felt 4½″ × 4½″ square 3½″ × 3½″ square 2½″ × 2½″ square	Bottom of tree Large Medium Small	Use pinking shears to cut: 1 piece using template D 1 piece using template E 1 piece using template F

FINDINGS: Machine sewing thread to match fabric, extra-strong polyester thread, 20-oz. bag premium polyester fiberfill

TOOLS: Sewing machine, clear template plastic, disappearing-ink fabric marker, pinking shears

Find Puffy Tabletop Christmas Trees Patterns A, B, C, D, E, and F on pullout page P2. Trace onto clear template plastic and cut out to create templates A, B, C, D, E, and F.

For more information about the supplies needed for this project, see My Sewing Necessities (page 14). For information about where to buy materials, see Resources (page 143).

Important

Super-strength polyester thread, such as Gütermann Extra-Strong Thread, is essential for this project. Do not substitute!

Puffy Tabletop Christmas Trees can add a forest of color to any holiday decor.

Getting It Together

TREE SPIKES

1. Fold circles in half, right sides together. Finger-press. Fold each circle again (into quarters), matching creases and raw edges. Finger-press. Open the last fold. You will have half-circles with a bisecting crease.

2. Using regular thread to match the fabric and a short stitch length (2.0), sew along the creased lines of all folded circles, backstitching at the beginning and end of each line. Cut the threads and trim.

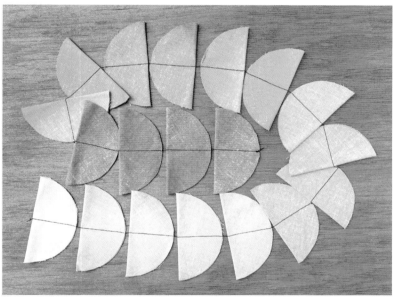

Chain-sew folded circles to save time.

3. Invert half of the circle over the other half to form a 2-layer fabric cone, right side out.

4. Thread a needle with at least 12″ of extra-strong thread. Backstitch (page 12), then use a ¼″ stitch to sew around the perimeter of the cone, ⅛″ from raw edges and through both layers of fabric.

Invert one side over the other to form double-walled cones.

5. Draw the thread up slightly and stuff each cone very firmly; think the firmness of a grape!

6. Draw up the thread to close the opening completely. Backstitch, knot, and trim the thread. Repeat the gathering and stuffing for the remaining cones.

Don't be stingy with the polyfill! Stuff cones firmly for a plump tree.

TREE ASSEMBLY

1. Thread a needle with an 18″ length of extra-strong thread and knot the end. Thread on 8 cones, taking a large (½″) stitch on the bottom of each cone.

Place all seams on the back side of your work so they won't show on the finished tree.

2. Move the cones to the center of the thread length and tie with a tight surgeon's knot (page 13). Press the cones as tightly as possible to each another.

3. Repeat Steps 1 and 2 for a second ring of 6 cones and a third ring of 4 cones. The remaining cone is for the top point of the tree.

All of the layers of a puffy tree ready to assemble

4. Place a ring of 8 cones, seams facedown, on a work surface. Place the set of 6 cones on top of the first, seams down, offsetting the cones as much as possible. Lift the second set off slightly and apply dots of hot glue where the cones touch. Be sparing. You can always add more glue. Press firmly until the glue cools.

5. Repeat Step 4 to add the third ring and the single top cone.

6. Apply hot glue to the back edges of the felt disc. Apply carefully to the bottom of the tree. Press the tree down on a flat surface until the glue is cool.

Glue pinked felt circle to base of tree.

Embellish!

- Sew or glue pompons to the tree tips.
- Tuck pompons between cones.
- Sew or pin beads onto the cone tips.

Furoshiki Gift-Card Box

FINISHED SIZE: 3½″ wide × 2½″ tall × 1¼″ deep
(fits a standard gift card)

Originating from Japanese culture, which promotes caring for the environment and reducing waste, furoshiki is the eco-friendly wrapping cloth. This project? A fun, reusable fabric-wrapping idea for a gift card or other small gift.

CONSTRUCTION OVERVIEW: Sandwich your favorite cotton quilting fabric with a stiff fusible interfacing. Fold the flaps in upon one another to hide a surprise!

Materials Requirements and Cutting Instructions

Furoshiki Gift-Card Box

FABRIC	FOR	CUTTING
Fat eighth or ¼ yard fabric	Outer box	Cut 1 rectangle 9″ × 12″.
Fat eighth or ¼ yard fabric	Inner box	Cut 1 rectangle 9″ × 12″.
9″ × 12″ rectangle or a heavy-duty double-sided fusible interfacing (I used Craf-Tex Plus. You also could use fast2fuse HEAVY.)	Interfacing	Cut 1 each from templates B, C, D, E, and F.

FINDINGS: Topstitching thread in colors that coordinate with the outer box fabric

TOOLS: Sewing machine, clear template plastic, iron, Fray Check, non-stick pressing sheet, gluestick

Find Furoshiki Gift-Card Box marking template A and Patterns B, C, D, E, and F on pullout page P2. Trace onto clear template plastic and cut out to create templates A, B, C, D, E, and F.

For more information about the supplies needed for this project, see My Sewing Necessities (page 14). For information about where to buy materials, see Resources (page 143).

The Furoshiki Gift-Card Box is a beautiful, reusable alternative to traditional wrapping for gift cards.

This box features the Early Bird Newspaper Cuttings for Collage by SUCH Designs for Windham.

This box features a Japanese novelty fabric.

This box features Small Susana from the Tana Lawn collection by Liberty Fabrics.

Getting It Together

1. Pin the outer and inner box fabrics, right sides together. Trace template A onto the back of the fabric.

2. Sew around the perimeter of the shape, directly on the drawn line. Leave an opening where indicated on the pattern. Clip the corners and curves. Reinforce all corners with Fray Check and let dry.

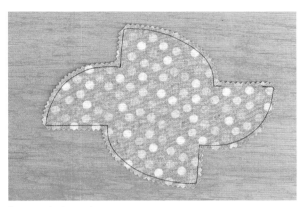

Sewn and trimmed

3. Use a gluestick to tack each interfacing shape to the corresponding space on the unit from Step 2, leaving an ⅛″ margin between the interfacing shapes and the stitching. This small margin will make it easier to fold the box. Let the glue dry.

4. Place the unit, interfacing side down, onto a nonstick pressing sheet. Press with a hot iron to fuse the interfacing to the fabric. Let cool.

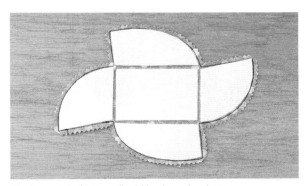

The heavy interfacing will add body to the shapes.

5. Turn the box right side out, using a turning tool to push out the corners. Use a ladder stitch (page 12) to close the opening. Press both sides with a hot iron to fuse interfacing to both fabrics.

6. Topstitch ⅛″ around the perimeter of the entire shape.

Topstitched box opened flat

7. To assemble, place a gift card onto the bottom rectangle. Fold the sides in 1 at a time, tucking straight sides under curved sides.

Folding in the flaps is as much fun as receiving this fun gift box!

Done!

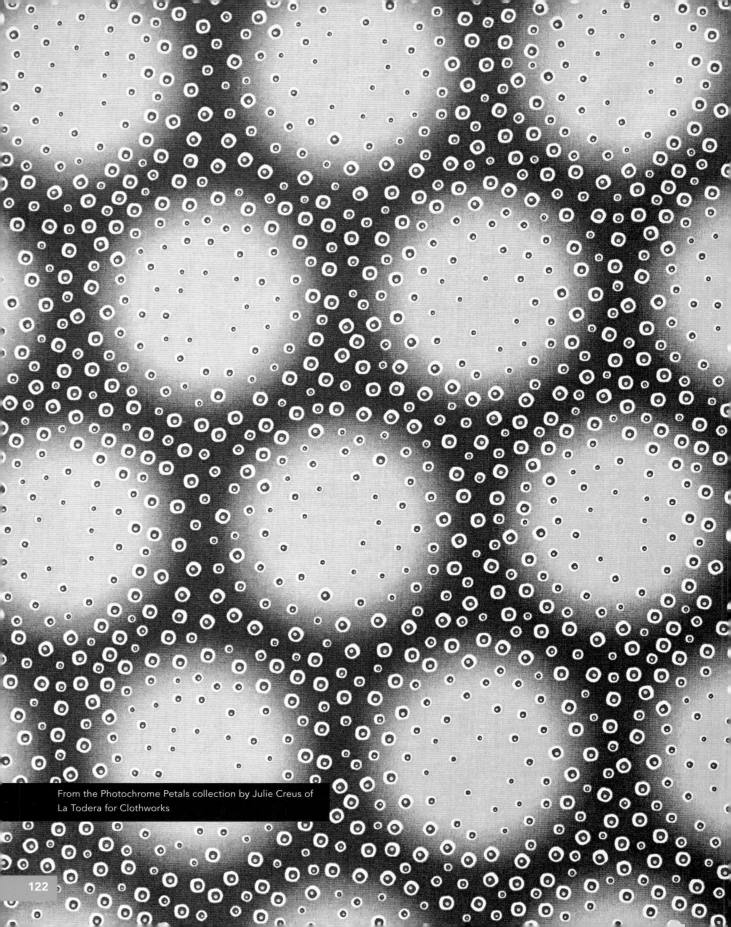

From the Photochrome Petals collection by Julie Creus of
La Todera for Clothworks

For the Kids' Area

Fabric is the perfect medium for accenting a child's environment. It's colorful, tactile, lightweight, and boo-boo proof! With the help of these projects, you can customize your kids' rooms to make their kingdom even cooler!

Of course, these projects are great for kids of *all* ages...

Grabby Tabs Ball

FINISHED SIZE: 12″ diameter

Great for little babies—and big babies too! Made of padded circles and stuffed with polyester fiberfill. Folded-back tabs give this ball pillow texture and make it easy to grab! And it is completely washable, which new parents will appreciate.

For this project, I used Suzani by Kaffe Fassett for Westminster Fabrics and Photochrome Petals by La Todera for Clothworks.

CONSTRUCTION OVERVIEW: Sew layers of fabric and fusible fleece to form 20 padded circles. Mark circles with triangle shapes. Join, sewing on lines to form a colorful polygon ball with tabs.

Materials Requirements and Cutting Instructions

Grabby Tabs Ball

FABRIC	FOR	CUTTING
1½ yards print	Outer ball	Cut 5 strips 8½˝ × width of fabric. Subcut into 20 squares 8½˝ × 8½˝.
1½ yards solid or contrasting print	Inner ball	Cut 5 strips 8½˝ × width of fabric. Subcut into 20 squares 8½˝ × 8½˝.
1½ yards fusible fleece, 45˝ wide (I used Bosal #325 Fusible Fleece.)	Interfacing	Cut 5 strips 8½˝ × width of fabric. Subcut into 20 squares 8½˝ × 8½˝.

FINDINGS: Variegated thread in coordinating color, 20-oz. bag basic polyester fiberfill

TOOLS: Sewing machine with walking foot, iron, clear template plastic, disappearing-ink fabric marker, pinking shears, regular sewing scissors

Find Grabby Tabs Ball marking templates A and B on pullout page P1. Trace onto clear template plastic and cut out to create templates A and B.

For more information about the supplies needed for this project, see My Sewing Necessities (page 14). For information about where to buy materials, see Resources (page 143).

The Grabby Tabs Ball is a colorful, easy-to-grab toy for children of any age. And it's washable, too!

Grabby Tabs Ball alternate colorway featuring Angelica from the Cameo collection by Amy Butler for Westminster and a fabric from my stash

Getting It Together

CIRCLE UNITS

1. Center template A on the wrong side of each inner ball fabric and trace with a fabric marker.

2. Make 5 stacks in the following order:

- Fusible fleece, with fusible (rough) side down

- Outer ball fabric, right side up

- Inner ball fabric, right side down

Pin.

3. Using a sewing machine with a walking foot, sew completely around the outline, directly on the drawn line.

Use your machine's walking foot to keep layers from shifting while you stitch.

4. Trim with pinking shears ¼″ away from the stitching.

5. With regular scissors, make a 1″ turning slit in the center of the top (inner ball) fabric only.

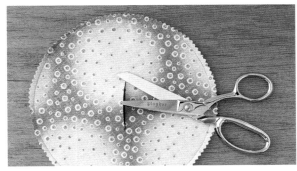

Cut the top layer only to make the turning slit.

6. Turn the padded circle right side out. Insert a chopstick or other blunt instrument through the slit and smooth the curves. Bring the edges of the turning slit together. Press to seal the edges, then press the entire unit to fuse the fabric completely to the fleece.

7. Topstitch each padded circle ¼″ from the edge.

Topstitch ¼″ from edge with variegated thread.

8. Place template B in the center of the top of each padded circle. The points of the triangle should be touching the line of topstitching. Trace with a disappearing-ink fabric marker.

Trace the marking template onto the right side of the padded circle.

ASSEMBLY

1. Pair 2 padded circles with the inner ball fabrics together. Match 2 sets of triangle points by pinning straight through a point on 1 circle to the point on the other side of the second circle to align. Affix the alignment with more pins, but leave the pins at the triangle points straight to keep the points accurately aligned.

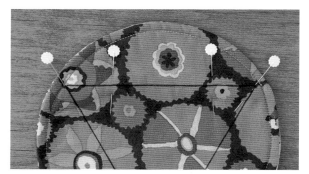

Pin straight through a point on the first circle to the other side of the second circle.

2. Sew on this line, backstitching at the beginning and end of the line. Do not sew past the topstitching to the outer edge of the circle. Clip all threads.

Sew directly on top of drawn template lines.

3. Place a third padded circle, inner sides together, with a paired circle. Repeat the pin alignment process from Step 1 and sew on the marked line.

A trio of fabric circles sewn together

Tip

To add circles 3 through 5, sew from the outer edge toward the bulky center. Take your time and use the walking foot on your machine.

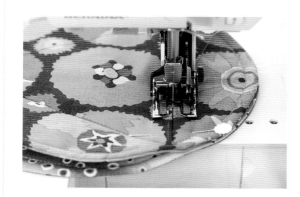

4. Add the fourth and fifth circles in the same manner.

One "pole" of the Grabby Tabs Ball.

5. Repeat Steps 1–4 to assemble another unit of 5 circles. Put the 2 sets aside.

6. To make the side strip, pair 2 circles as in Steps 2 and 3 and sew the first line. Add 8 more circles, but instead of sewing them together into a central point, sew them into a long strip.

On the first and last circles, topstitch the remaining unsewn triangle sides. The top stitching will help the stuffing opening keep its shape and look like the rest of the seams after being hand-sewn shut later.

The "equator" of the ball coming together. Note the zigzag pattern.

7. Join the ends of the strip, sewing directly on the topstitching done in Step 6, but leaving a 3″ opening in the center of the seam for stuffing.

The "equator" section finished and ready to attach to the "poles" of the ball

8. Pin the side strip to the top set, matching the points of the triangles. Join sections 1 at a time in 2 steps, this time sewing from the center of each pair toward a bulky intersection, removing pins as you sew. Next, go back to the center and sew forward toward the remaining intersection. Backstitch at each end.

Add the bottom of the ball to the center section in the same manner.

9. Stuff the ball firmly with small handfuls of polyester fiberfill. Sew the opening shut using a ladder stitch (page 12) directly on top of the top stitching created in Step 6.

10. Press each set of flaps open lightly.

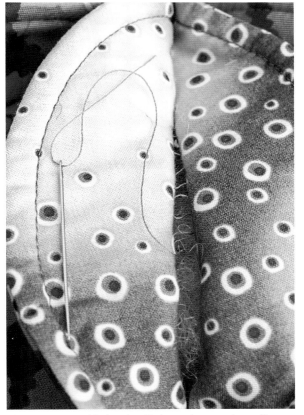

All sections assembled and stuffed. Hand sewing the stuffing opening on top of the faux top stitching makes the closing virtually invisible.

Done!

Llama Mama and Baby

FINISHED SIZE: Mama: 20˝ wide × 28˝ tall × 2˝ thick;
Baby: 12˝ wide × 18˝ tall × 2˝ thick

These llamas are a nod to my years in Argentina. There are llamas a-go-go in the northern regions. Mom is in a tranquil sitting position, while baby is standing up and ready to play! Made of 2½˝ squares and fusible grid, these guys are a snap to put together. Flower eyes remind me of the llamas' looong eyelashes!

For this project, I used mostly scraps of Kaffe Fassett Collective for Westminster Fabrics and Photochrome Petals by La Todera for Clothworks.

CONSTRUCTION OVERVIEW: Fuse 2½˝ fabric squares to a fusible grid outline. Sew seams and join sides with a gusset. Stuff and add button eyes layered with silk flowers.

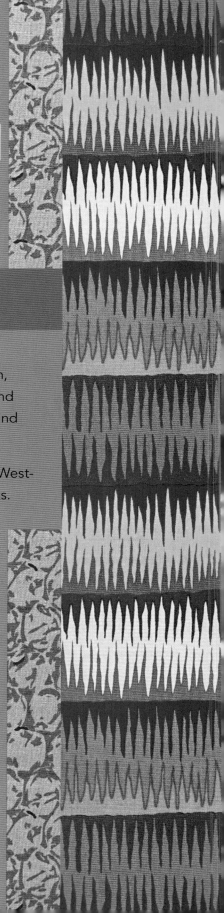

Materials Requirements and Cutting Instructions

Llama Mama and Baby

FABRIC	FOR	CUTTING
Precut strip bundle containing at least 20 strips 2½″ × width of fabric to make both llamas Or Assorted charm squares 5″ × 5″ (You will need at least 53 charm squares for mama and 24 squares for baby.)	Llama side panels and gussets	Subcut into squares 2½″ × 2½″. You will need 210 squares for Mama Llama and 90 for Baby Llama.
2¼ yards fusible 2½″ (2″ finished) grid for mama, 1¼ yards for baby (I used 2½″ Fusible Grid by Bosal, 42″ wide.) **Note:** If you cannot find fusible grid, use a thin fusible nonwoven interfacing and draw a 2½″ grid with a ruler and fine permanent marker. Buy twice the amount of interfacing because it is usually only 22″ wide.	Sewing base	Mark and cut according to project directions.

FINDINGS: 1″ buttons and silk flowers, petal layers removed from plastic flower center, extra-strong thread, turning tool, 20-oz. bag basic polyester fiberfill

TOOLS: Sewing machine with walking foot; iron; fine-point permanent marker; narrow, sharp scissors; rotary cutter, ruler, and mat

For more information about the supplies needed for this project, see My Sewing Necessities (page 14). For information about where to buy materials, see Resources (page 143).

My official and mighty-picky panel of (household kid) testers say they love the long necks on the Llama Mama and Baby—easy to grab and carry around!

Getting It Together
SIDE PANELS AND GUSSET

All seams are ¼″.

1. Place the fusible grid, printed side up, over a white surface, such as paper, fabric, or a white countertop, so that you can easily see the grid. Following the pattern-marking diagrams (below), use a fine-point permanent marker to draw the outline of your chosen size of llama, as well as the gusset strips. Use a clear ruler and follow the preprinted gridlines to help you draw straight lines. Cut out llama and gusset shapes following the marked gridlines.

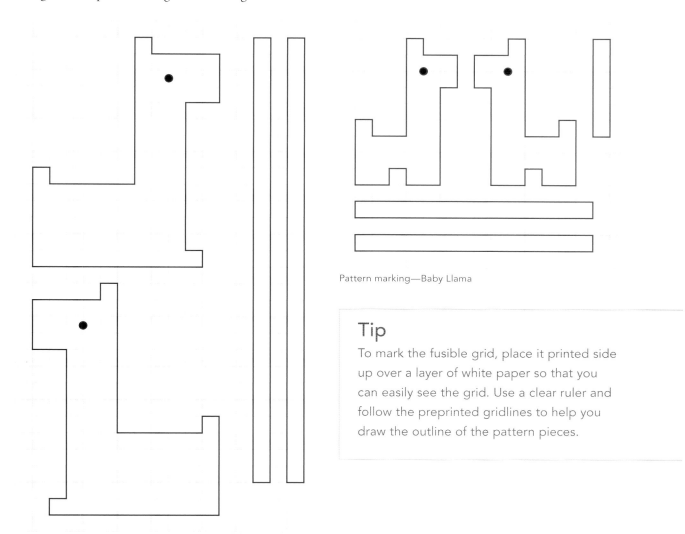

Pattern marking—Baby Llama

Tip
To mark the fusible grid, place it printed side up over a layer of white paper so that you can easily see the grid. Use a clear ruler and follow the preprinted gridlines to help you draw the outline of the pattern pieces.

Pattern marking—Mama Llama

2. Place a llama shape fusible side up. Arrange the fabric squares, faceup, as neatly as possible within the gridlines.

Tip

Be as neat as you can, but know that small discrepancies will not show in your finished llama since you will be sewing on the fusible grid and not the fabric.

3. Using a sheet of white paper as a "pressing cloth," gently fuse the squares onto the fusible grid with a dry iron on the cotton setting.

Use a piece of paper under the iron to keep it from sticking to the fusible grid.

Critical

Change your iron to the synthetic setting at this point so that you do not melt the fusible grid in later steps.

4. At each vertical seam, fold the grid inward (fabric sides together) along marked lines and finger-press. Sew, backstitching at the beginning and end of the seam, enclosing the edges of the fabric.

Important

Set your machine to a short stitch length, such as 2 on a scale of 0 to 5. This will prevent the fiberfill from escaping later. Use a walking foot if the fusible grid slips under your presser foot.

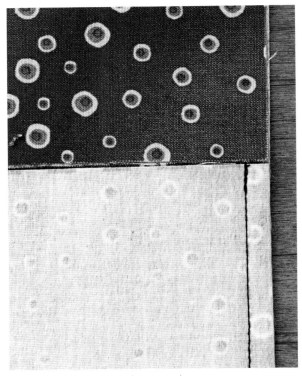

A vertical seam, with a single square above

5. Slit all seams open with narrow, sharp scissors. Press seams open with an iron set on the Synthetic setting. Around the perimeter of the llama shape, a few points in the seams will prevent the fabric from lying flat. Simply clip the offending half of each of those seams up to the sewing line. Press the panel again on the fabric side.

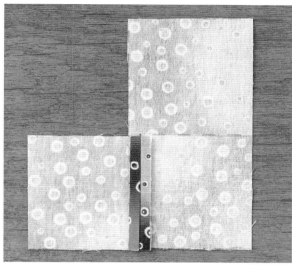

Slit the fusible grid and press seams open.

6. Repeat Steps 4 and 5 for all horizontal seams. Pause to admire your crisp, perfect seams!

Finished llama panel. Your seams were never so perfect!

7. Repeat Steps 4–6 to make the other side panel of the llama.

8. For the gusset, fuse fabric squares onto the gusset strips.

9. Sew the gusset strips together to form a continuous loop, then sew all gusset seams *but do not backstitch*. (See why in Step 2 of Llama Assembly, page 136.) Slit the seams open and press.

Completed gusset loop

LLAMA ASSEMBLY

1. Beginning at the head section of the back panel of the llama, start pinning the gusset to the side panel, right sides together and matching seams. The gusset strip will be the top side of your work. Backstitch and begin sewing the gusset to the body.

Apply the gusset to the first side of the llama. Use lots of pins; they won't hurt her.

2. When you reach an outside corner, stop sewing at the seam of the gusset strip (¼˝ from the edge of the side panel). Backstitch and remove your work from the machine. Pivot the strip, then pin and begin sewing ¼˝ from the edge. Continue to the next corner, backstitching at both ends of the seam.

Technical marvel

Because gusset seams were not backstitched in previous steps, they will handily split a bit at corners, making maneuvering the gusset easier.

Pivot the outside corners of the gusset to align with the llama side panel.

3. At inside corners, sew up to the seam, then backstitch and remove from the machine. Pivot the strip, then pin and sew to the next corner, backstitching at both ends of the seam. Fold excess gusset fabric out of the way as you sew.

Pivoting at an inside corner of the gusset

4. Continue stitching the gusset to the llama shape, sewing completely around the perimeter.

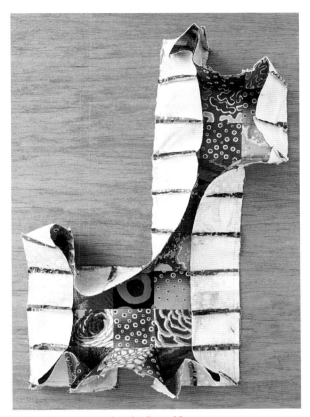

Adding the gusset makes the llama 3D.

5. Use the same process to stitch the other side panel to the remaining edge of the gusset strip. This time, begin on the hind section of the llama, leaving a 3″ hind section unsewn for stuffing.

6. Turn the llama right side out and push out the corners with a turning tool. Press the gusset seams.

7. Stuff the llama with small handfuls of polyester fiberfill. Start with the tail and ear, stuffing the main body last.

8. Use matching thread to ladder stitch (page 12) the opening closed.

9. For "flower eyes," layer a button over 1 or more layers of a silk flower. Sew on button eyes with heavy thread at the points indicated in the pattern marking diagrams (page 133).

Fluttery silk flower eyes add enchantment and, curiously, authenticity! Llamas are known for their fantastic eyelashes!

Done. Can you hear the Andean flutes playing in the background?

Butterfly Bunting

FINISHED SIZE OF BUTTERFLIES:
Large: 16″ × 8½″ tall × ¾″ deep; Small: 10″ wide × 5½″ tall × ½″ deep

Hang them in rows on a ribbon, or stick them on a wall in groups!
And there is a bonus—when finished with the butterfly bunting
display, simply peel off the freezer paper to repurpose the fabric!
Adorn a kiddie room, a birthday party, or maybe the classroom of
a very special teacher!

For this project, I used Photochrome Petals by La Todera for
Clothworks.

CONSTRUCTION OVERVIEW: Make with fabric fused to
freezer paper, cut to shape, and pleated. Alternating sizes are
attached to a grosgrain ribbon.

Materials Requirements and Cutting Instructions

Butterfly Bunting

FABRIC	FOR	CUTTING
½ yard fabric	Large butterfly	Cut into 17″ × 26″ rectangle.
⅜ yard or fat quarter of fabric	Small butterfly	Cut into 11″ × 17″ rectangle.

FINDINGS: Freezer-paper roll; ¼″-wide grosgrain ribbon; thin wire, twist ties, or pipe cleaner in coordinating colors; regular sewing thread that matches butterfly fabric

TOOLS: Sewing machine, iron, craft scissors, pinking shears, gluestick, straight pins or stapler, template plastic

Find Butterfly Bunting Large and Small Patterns on pullout page P1. Follow project directions for tracing and cutting templates to create Large and Small templates.

For more information about the supplies needed for the project, see My Sewing Necessities (page 14). For information about where to buy materials, see Resources (page 143).

Getting It Together

BASIC BUTTERFLY CONSTRUCTION

1. The pattern drawn is half of a butterfly. Place template plastic over the pattern, making sure to leave room to rotate and trace the second half. Trace the first half onto template plastic. Flip the template plastic and rotate 180°. Trace the other half of the butterfly. (*Note: Half of the butterfly will be on 1 side of the template and the other half will be on the other side.*) Cut out. Trace the outline of the large or small pattern onto the nonshiny side of freezer paper. With craft scissors, cut out roughly around the outline, leaving at least a ½″ margin.

The Butterfly Bunting, featuring two sizes of butterflies, adds a festive air to any decor or occasion. Butterflies look fantastic in groups applied directly to a wall. Simply mount with double-stick foam tape or sew a loop of heavy thread on the back of the butterfly. See Folded Wall Flowers, Finishing (page 41).

2. With a pencil, start at the bottom of each butterfly shape and draw lines every ¾″ across the width of the large butterfly shape or every ½″ for the small butterfly.

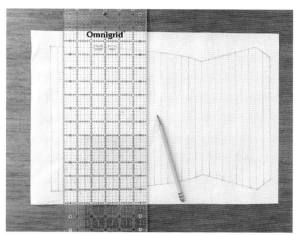

Trace the shape onto freezer paper and add fold lines in pencil.

3. Fuse freezer paper, shiny side down, to the wrong side of fabric with a hot, dry iron. If the fabric has a large print, be sure to position the butterfly outline symmetrically. Cut around the butterfly outline with pinking shears.

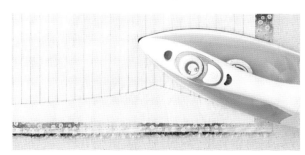

Iron freezer paper onto the back of the fabric.

4. Fan-fold the shape on the pencil lines, starting at the top of the form. The first fold should be paper to paper. Finger-crease each fold.

5. When you have finished folding, press the shape together tightly and set the creases lightly with an iron.

6. Repeat Steps 2–5 to make as many butterflies as you wish.

BUNTING ASSEMBLY

1. Plan the arrangement and length of the bunting, leaving at least 6″ between butterflies and at least 24″ of ribbon at each end for tying.

2. Fold the top flap of the butterfly shape over the ribbon. Use a bit of gluestick to secure, then machine stitch with matching thread.

Attach each butterfly to the ribbon.

FINISHING DETAILS

1. Cinch each butterfly in the center with a short length of wire twist tie or pipe cleaner. Trim extra wire or form into antennae if desired.

2. Measure from the center a third to halfway down the wings and use a straight pin or staple to secure the lower butterfly wings together from the back side of the last fold.

Cinch the center of each butterfly with wire and pin the bottom wings together.

Voilà! Done!

About the Author

Photo by The Picture People, Orlando, Florida

JULIE CREUS is an artist born in Illinois, where many of her foremothers were seamstresses and quilters.

She studied graphic design and fashion merchandising back in the Stone Age at the University of Illinois, then promptly changed careers upon graduation, much to the chagrin of her parental units. It wasn't until 2008, when she started designing soft craft and quilt patterns, that those skills (investments!) finally began to pay off.

In 1993, she fell in love with an Argentine and Argentina. After a six-month long-distance courtship, she sold almost everything she owned (except her sewing machine) and moved herself, her cat, and seven suitcases to South America. She lived in Buenos Aires, Argentina, for nine years in a beautiful historic brownstone with patterned tile on the floor and a giant camellia tree in the backyard.

It was there that she joined a small quilt group, and it was *amor* at first stitch. She found her fellow artists in Argentina to be cultured and extremely resourceful, and those influences continue to shape her work to this day. It was there that her good friend Cecilia gave her the name *la todera* (a female jack-of-all-trades) and later encouraged her to share her sewing and craft patterns with the world.

Julie's Midwestern upbringing steered her to create versatile, durable, practical projects. But her years in Argentina honed her skills to create unique, stylish items with clever construction methods.

Julie says that the only thing better than crafting is sharing the knowledge! She loves to teach classes, write patterns, and design fabrics, and she is super *emocionada* about this book!

Resources

The first place to go for information and products is your local quilt shop. If that is not possible or they cannot help you, then try the Internet.

ONLINE QUILT SHOPS

eQuilter online quilt store | equilter.com

Hancock's of Paducah Fabrics | hancocks-paducah.com

Glorious Color Fabrics and Kaffe Fassett Grey Design Wall Flannel Fabric | gloriouscolor.com

Sew It Up quilt shop | sewitup.com

The Sewing Studio | sewing.net

The Quilt Asylum | thequiltasylum.com

FABRICS

Note: Fabrics used in the quilts shown may not be currently available, as fabric manufacturers keep most fabrics in print for only a short time.

Windham Fabrics/Marcia Derse Designs | windhamfabrics.com

Art Gallery Fabrics/Pat Bravo Designs | artgalleryfabrics.com

Clothworks/Julie Creus at La Todera | clothworks.com

E.E. Schenck/Importer of Gelato Fabrics | eeschenck.com

Westminster/Rowan Fabrics/Kaffe Fassett, Brandon Mably, Amy Butler Designs | westminsterfabrics.com

Robert Kaufman Fabrics | robertkaufman.com

Liberty Fabrics | liberty.co.uk

Michael Miller Fabrics | michaelmillerfabrics.com

Kona Bay Fabrics | konabay.com

Moda Fabrics | modabakeshop.com

Free Spirit Fabric | freespiritfabric.com

Yuwa Fabrics | yuwafabrics.e-biss.jp

FUSIBLES AND FILLINGS

Bosal Interfacings
bosalfoam.com

Fairfield Fiberfill Products
fairfieldworld.com

Heat*n*Bond Fusibles
thermoweb.com

Pellon Interfacings
shoppellon.com

THREADS

Aurifil | www.aurifil.com

Gutermann Threads
gutermann-thread.com

OTHER

Flat Flower Head Pins
dritz.com

Olfa Mats, Cutters, and Rulers
olfa.com

Bernina Sewing Machines
bernina.com

stashBOOKS®

fabric arts for a handmade lifestyle

If you're craving beautiful authenticity in a time of mass-production...Stash Books is for you. Stash Books is a line of how-to books celebrating fabric arts for a handmade lifestyle. Backed by C&T Publishing's solid reputation for quality, Stash Books will inspire you with contemporary designs, clear and simple instructions, and engaging photography.

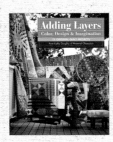

www.ctpub.com